Classic American Costume Jewelry

IDENTIFICATION & VALUE GUIDE

Jacqueline Rehmann

COLLECTOR BOOKS
A Division of Schroeder Publishing Co., Inc.

Front Cover: top right, Coro enamel flower brooch, 2½" long, ⬛⬛⬛⬛⬛ stic bracelet, 7½", unsigned, $20.00 – 30.00. Fan-shaped brooch, signed ©HAR, $100.00 – 125.00. Heart-shaped matte gold-tone and enamel brooch, 2½" at its widest, named "Heart of Hollywood," signed ELIZABETH TAYLOR across the top, AVON across the bottom, and a capital E in script between the two, $125.00 – 150.00 (price is for brooch and earrings). Orange, yellow, and green enameled flower brooch, 2½" in diameter, unsigned, $35.00 – 50.00 (price is for brooch and earrings). Gold-tone and pearl tree, signed MARVELLA© on a raised circle, $35.00 – 50.00. Petite ballerina, 1½" tall, unsigned, $20.00 – 35.00 (price is for brooch and coordinating earrings). Enameled trim necklace, marked Coro without the copyright symbol and PAT PEND with other illegible letters or numbers, $40.00 – 65.00 (price is for necklace and matching earrings).

Back Cover: top right, Fox brooch, unsigned, $30.00 – 45.00. Brooch features gold-tone leaves and huge center unfoiled rhinestone with an open back, 2" across, unsigned, probably made by DeLizza and Elster, $75.00 – 100.00. Adjustable necklace features leaf-shaped plastic inserts accented with aurora borealis rhinestones in a silver-tone setting, signed LISNER, $35.00 – 50.00. Rectangular-shaped clip earrings, unsigned, $20.00 – 30.00. Brooch featuring a rose cut faux smoky topaz, 3½" from top to bottom, signed FLORENZA©, $50.00 – 65.00. Enamel mandolin in an almost-olive green color accented with iridescent green and pink stripes, signed KARU Arké INC., $35.00 – 50.00 (price is for brooch and matching earrings). High quality enameled brooch with mauve and aurora borealis rhinestones, signed SELINI©, $75.00 – 100.00.

Cover design: Beth Summers • Book design: Lisa Henderson • Cover photography: Charles R. Lynch

COLLECTOR BOOKS
P.O. Box 3009
Paducah, Kentucky 42002–3009
www.collectorbooks.com

Copyright © 2009 Jacqueline Rehmann

All rights reserved. No part of this book may be reproduced, stored in any retrieval system, or transmitted in any form, or by any means including but not limited to electronic, mechanical, photocopy, recording, or otherwise, without the written consent of the author or publisher.

The current values in this book should be used only as a guide. They are not intended to set prices, which vary from one section of the country to another. Auction prices as well as dealer prices vary greatly and are affected by condition as well as demand. Neither the author nor the publisher assumes responsibility for any losses that might be incurred as a result of consulting this guide.

Searching for a Publisher?

We are always looking for people knowledgeable within their fields. If you feel that there is a real need for a book on your collectible subject and have a large comprehensive collection, contact Collector Books.

Proudly printed and bound in the United States of America

Contents

Dedication 4

Acknowledgments 4

About the Author 5

Outline of the Book 7

Introduction 8

Fashion and Jewelry Timeline 19

Brooches 26

Demi Parures and Parues 102

Necklaces 141

Bracelets 147

Earrings 153

Children As Collectors 157

Selected Costume Jewelry Designers and Manufacturers . 161

Bibliography 190

Index 192

Dedication

This book is dedicated to the men and women who designed and manufactured the jewelry described throughout. Their unique and creative genius endowed us with the art form now known as vintage costume jewelry. Without them this book could not have been written.

Acknowledgments

Many wonderful people helped make this project a reality.

It really all started a long time ago. My parents patiently instilled in their children a love of beautiful old things by taking us along on their antique buying excursions and educating us about the items they collected. Today, we are all collectors of one thing or another. My mother is my companion on buying expeditions and we enjoy the chase as much as the catch. She is particularly adept at finding beautiful jewelry. She was the one who spotted the Miriam Haskell brooch featured in this book. She also insisted that I buy it. I needed no encouragement!

My husband has encouraged me every step of the way in this project. He rolled up his sleeves to serve as the photographer. Considering the number of photographs (not to mention retakes!), it is easy to see why this project would not have happened without him.

My children have offered lively encouragement and support. My daughter has become my collecting companion. She is the cautious shopper, putting items back that don't meet her high standards. My son has been patient while I've spent hours reading and writing and he has learned a few things too. He recently pointed out a brooch at a flea market and said I should buy it because it was a "jelly belly." Hmmm, little ears…

My sister helped me with the research for this book. Her unbounded enthusiasm and love has provided constant encouragement. Her efforts to collect information on vintage costume jewelry have spanned more than a year. As a librarian, she enjoys the challenge of finding new information about old subjects. She is a real pro.

My friends, Maria and Lois, have provided love and encouragement to me through many chapters of my life. They share my passion for vintage costume jewelry and have given me several pieces. Some of their gifts are featured in this book.

My aunt has given me some lovely pieces of vintage costume jewelry through the years. Her pretty pieces have helped me learn to look carefully for marks and signatures.

I have met many people who have generously offered information about the lovely items they collect and sell. In particular I would like to thank Pat Seal. Our e-mail exchanges and telephone conversations have been encouraging and educational. Thank you, Pat, for being so supportive of this project. Pat and Dotty Stringfield are the architects of the invaluable website www.illusionjewels.com/costumejewelrymarks.html which I and many jewelry collectors use all the time.

Last but not least, I'd like to thank Ruth Uhde for giving me several pieces of costume jewelry. In particular, the pieces from the Order of the Eastern Star are from Ruth.

About the Author

Most collectors remember the first piece of jewelry they bought as though it happened yesterday. I am one of them. But before I tell you about my first purchase, I must tell you the story about the first time I wore a piece of costume jewelry. I was nine years old and in fourth grade. Our parents were encouraged to visit the classroom and observe their children. For this special day my mother let me wear her gold costume jewelry bracelet that had one large dangling pearl. I was captivated by this bracelet. When answering a question in class, I raised only that hand. When my parents came to class, I waved with that hand. What a great day that was! I was so proud that my parents were there and I was wearing the most beautiful bracelet in the world! Unfortunately, the bracelet has been mislaid over the years and we cannot find it.

Two years later, I bought my first vintage costume accessory. Our family was on vacation in Vermont where we were visiting friends. One afternoon, I tended their antique shop while they ran an errand and that's when I saw it — a champleve buckle with a red stone. The buckle is shown below. I used the dollar I earned that day to buy the buckle. It was the first of many dollars that I would spend on costume jewelry! Sometime later I purchased a brooch at my church's yard sale. I paid a pittance for the brooch below. In the ensuing 40 years, I have purchased jewelry everywhere — at antique shops, flea markets, clothing consignment shops, and thrift shops. My collection has been enriched by many family pieces. When my aunt was cleaning out her home and preparing to move into an assisted-living community, she gave me several pieces of her costume jewelry. They are featured in this book. One of my favorite brooches from my aunt is shown on the top left of page 6. My mother has given me several pieces that have special memories. These I will treasure forever. The Eugene brooch shown at the top right of page 6 is one of her favorites. My sister and brother-in-law gave me some lovely pieces of his mother's, including a Coro duette shown on the bottom of the

Jacqueline Rehmann, author, and her husband, Robert Lacovara. Photo by Liz Wuillerman.

Champleve buckle with glued-in red center stone. The stone is a recent replacement. Champleve is an enameling technique in which areas of metal are cut or etched and filled with enamel. It was most commonly applied to copper or bronze. Unsigned, $35.00 – 50.00.

A real bargain at 25 cents! I purchased this unsigned brooch at a church flea market. Its beauty has not diminished during the 40 years I have owned it. Present value, $20.00 – 30.00.

About the Author

page and a Schreiner brooch shown on the top of the next page.

The internet has provided yet another venue to purchase a variety of costume jewelry. Between eBay and online dealers, collectors have unprecedented access to a remarkable amount and variety of lovely items.

The appreciation of beautiful things begins slowly and the seeds are planted in us when we are young. Today I continue to collect vintage costume jewelry with my ten year old daughter. She is learning the basics of collecting by accompanying me on buying trips. Using her magnifying glass she is quite capable of identifying signatures, finding loose stones, and detecting metal loss and breakage. She has already built a small collection of jewelry. Someday I hope she will tell the story of her first purchase of vintage costume jewelry.

This large brooch features a gold-tone setting with plastic inserts and purple rhinestone trim. The blue plastic is molded to look like feathers; the blue enamel on the toucan's tail is dotted with clear rhinestones as is the bird's perch. The beak is a pretty ivory colored plastic. I have often seen this brooch described as an unsigned Hattie Carnegie piece. The style and quality is certainly consistent with other figural jewelry made by Hattie Carnegie. Unsigned, $100.00 – 125.00.

This lovely gold-tone pin with pearl accents belonged to my mother before she gave it to me. She often wore this pin as evidenced by the signs of wear including some of the pearls which have lost their nacre. The pin has a bail and can be worn as a pendant; the brooch originally came with a matching chain. With the chain missing and some signs of wear, the value of this item to a collector would be reduced. Signed Eugene on an oval cartouche. $35.00 – 50.00.

Pretty duette photographed unassembled to reveal the mechanism. It is marked Coro Duette and Pat. 1798867. This utility patent is dated March 31, 1931, and was issued to Gaston Candas. The clips attach to the frame so they can be worn as a brooch; unassembled they are worn as dress clips. The utility patent protected the design of the duette mechanism. $125.00 – 150.00.

Captivating crescent-shaped Schreiner brooch; note the large flower which is the focal point of the brooch accented by smaller flowers. The brooch is signed SCHREINER NEW YORK on an oval cartouche. $175.00 – 200.00.

Schreiner jewelry is very collectible because it was made by hand using high quality materials. Characteristics of Schreiner jewelry include inverted and unfoiled rhinestones, large faceted stones in irregular shapes, and decorative prongs. It is difficult to find and is usually expensive when you can find it.

Outline of the Book

Introduction
When I use the term vintage costume jewelry, I am referring to twentieth century jewelry made with mostly non-precious materials. This section describes many important aspects for vintage costume jewelry enthusiasts to consider, especially when they are beginning to collect. Many of the anecdotes in this section are based upon my experiences. Photographs of vintage costume jewelry are used to illustrate the points being made. Included in this book are pieces of jewelry that are at least 20 years old with a few exceptions.

Fashion and Jewelry Timeline
This section provides a detailed timeline of jewelry trends as well as the history that helped shape them as described in magazine and newspaper columns of the day. Selected twentieth century events that affected the evolution of costume jewelry are described as well.

Vintage Costume Jewelry Photographs and Descriptions
These chapters contain most of the photographs in this book. Interesting historical anecdotes are included as well as selected vintage ads. Each piece of jewelry is assigned an average value based upon a combination of extensive research, current selling prices on eBay, and dealers' prices as found in antique shops and online markets. Chapters include: (1) brooches, (2) demi parures and parures, (3) necklaces, (4) bracelets, and (5) earrings. Photographs of signed and unsigned vintage jewelry are accompanied by detailed descriptions.

Children as Collectors
This section features the modest but growing collection of my daughter.

Selected Costume Jewelry Designers and Manufacturers
Makers, dates of operation, marks, and design characteristics are featured in table format. The table contains information on the jewelry makers and designers whose work I feature. I have gathered information from many sources as reflected in the bibliography.

Introduction

I think of vintage costume jewelry as the perfect collectible. The abundance and variety of vintage costume jewelry provides something for everyone's taste and budget. A collection can be specialized, targeting a specific designer or manufacturer; or it can be theme-based, focusing on Christmas jewelry or enamel flower pins. Whatever your taste, collecting vintage costume jewelry is enjoyable, interesting, affordable, and educational.

Antique collectors are challenged to find adequate space to store and display their collections. With jewelry, this challenge is minimized. I have several hundred pieces comfortably settled in one highboy in my bedroom and I can enjoy my treasures by simply pulling out a drawer. I have spent many pleasant hours sorting, cleaning, and organizing my collection. I periodically take out selected pieces to exhibit in glass-front display cases.

The beauty of vintage costume jewelry is irresistible. Many of the large costume jewelry makers looked to styles and designs of fine jewelry for inspiration when making their more affordable counterparts. Marcel Boucher and Kenneth Jay Lane are but two examples among many designers. Each added unique touches. Kenneth Jay Lane's copies possess a style and scale that make them instantly recognizable as his own. Alfred Philippe, a designer for Trifari for over 40 years, worked for Cartier and Van Cleef and Arpels before joining Trifari. Marcel Boucher apprenticed at Cartier before going out on his own. Ironically, by the 1940s costume jewelry was so popular and selling so well it often served as the inspiration for jewelry made with real gold and gems!

The artistry and skill of costume jewelry designers and manufacturers resulted in many beautiful designs including the fantastic and friendly creatures associated with ART, HAR, and Hobé. In my opinion, there is simply no description or photograph that can prepare one for the luminous beauty of the HAR fantasy pieces. The photo on the top right shows a detail of a HAR dragon bracelet. Perhaps the mystery of this company adds to the allure but I don't think so. The pieces themselves are simply captivating.

Jewelry as Art

Vintage costume jewelry contains many of the design elements of fine paintings or sculpture. Brilliant and subtle use of materials, color, and design transform ordinary materials into a beautiful gestalt. This was no accident. There are many examples of artists who worked as jewelry designers. One of the most well-known is McClelland Barclay who worked as a graphic artist. His drawings appeared on the covers of magazines and in many ads throughout the 1930s. During the early 1940s he even created recruitment posters for the U.S. armed forces. One of his posters is shown in Figure 1. He was a member of the U.S. Naval Reserve on active duty when, tragically, he was killed in 1943. His beautiful and well-made jewelry pieces are distinctive, rare, and highly collectible. A typical McClelland Barclay brooch is shown on the right. Is it any wonder his jewelry is so highly sought after?

Collectors consider McClelland Barclay jewelry to be among the best costume jewelry ever made. The classic designs and superior

Detail of HAR dragon clamper bracelet. Note the flaring nostrils on the dragon who appears ready to spew forth fire. Signed HAR©. $500.00 – 750.00.

Classic brooch measures 1¾" x 2" and is signed McClelland Barclay. It features a heavy gold-tone setting with red prong-set rhinestones surrounded by clear stones. A truly stunning piece. $250.00 – 300.00.

Introduction: Jewelry as Art

Figure 1. Copy of WWII recruitment poster by McClelland Barclay.

In 1935 Alberto Giacometti designed surreal ornaments for Schiaparelli's salon at 21 Place Vendome in Paris. After 1945 several painters and sculptors designed jewelry. One of the most successful was Alexander Calder who made simple ornaments of forged metal. In 1965 Yves Saint Laurent based an entire fashion collection on the work of the Dutch artist Piet Mondrian (1872 – 1944). Mondrian used primary colors, along with gray and black to create his geometric forms. Some of the HAR fruit and butterfly brooches more than suggest the geometric paintings of Mondrian (see bottom left photo). In the late 1960s Jonas Eisenberg began the manufacture of enameled jewelry made in various figural designs and inspired by the artwork of different artists, including Pablo Picasso. The photo on the bottom right shows an example of this jewelry. The jewelry of Elsa Schiaparelli continued to be heavily influenced by Dadaism and Surrealism. The leading proponents of these movements were close friends of hers and included Salvador Dali, Jean Cocteau, and Christian Berard. The inspiration for her "Shocking Pink" collection of 1936 was Surrealism.

Costume jewelry was legally recognized as art when in 1955, a Federal judge ruled that costume jewelry designs were "works of art" and should be accorded the protection of U.S. copyright laws (Trifari v. Charel). After this date, the copyright symbol generally appeared on jewelry. Coro, however, began using the copyright symbol much earlier, perhaps as early as 1947.

quality materials distinguish these lovely pieces. His sterling pieces are beautifully made and highly collectible. Unfortunately, they have been reproduced.

There are many other examples of artists who designed jewelry or whose artwork inspired designs. Hattie Carnegie jewelry was designed for a time by Nadine Effront. Ms. Effront was a French sculptress and former student of the great cubist Georges Braque. In

Apple-shaped enameled pin in shades of blue in a design reminiscent of the paintings of Dutch artist Piet Mondrian. It is signed ©HAR. $35.00 – 50.00.

Enamel stick pin with matching earrings, inspired by the work of Cubist artists Georges Braque and Pablo Picasso. Shown on original cards with tags, the set is 18K gold electro plated metal and enamel. It is signed EISENBERG© on a raised rectangle. The tag reads "hand painted Eisenberg Enamels." This set is from the early 1970s. $85.00 – 110.00.

Introduction: Art Imitates Life

Art Imitates Life

Vintage costume jewelry designs and materials reflect the history of the era in which they were used. The lovely large brooches known as Retro Modern are an excellent example of history in the making. By May of 1942, the costume jewelry industry stopped manufacturing goods using banned metals from a long list issued by the War Protection Board. Thus, costume jewelry made during this period was often made of sterling silver and marked accordingly, helping to date these lovely and historic pieces.

Other materials were used as well. The extraordinary Elzac pieces produced during the 1940s reveal what could be done with ordinary substances including felt, plastic, and string. Even buttons and head-dress ornaments were being made of pine cones, baked porcelain, and horse hair and were referred to as "the whimsical step-children of priority rulings" in a *New York Times* fashion column of the day.[1]

I Should Wear It Where?

Many collectors regularly wear pieces of jewelry from their collection. I worked in an office for many years and on most days wore a business suit. I received many compliments on my jewelry because the pieces were unique and unusual. Ordinary business attire accented by one-of-a-kind jewelry has a style all its own.

The transformation could be aided by clever placement of a brooch or string of pearls. Elizabeth Taylor, in her book entitled *My Love Affair with Jewelry* is shown wearing fabulous pieces from her stunning collection of real gems. She would wear a brooch in her hair, to hold a scarf in place high upon her shoulder, or at the small of her back. A few years later some of her lovely jewels would serve as inspiration for her line of costume jewelry for Avon.

Over the years, many designers gave instructions for how their creations should be worn and often intended "double lives" for their designs. Necklaces as belts and brooches as hat, purse, or shoe accents were common creative uses of jewelry through the decades. Fashion icon Coco Chanel abandoned convention by layering strings of pearls and gobs of faux jewel-encrusted bangle bracelets. Years ahead of her time, Ms. Chanel was heaping it on in the 1920s! Joseff of Hollywood once noted that jewelry would draw the eye to where it is placed. To show off a small waistline, he recommended wearing a brooch at the waist. In 1953, the *New York Times* reported that tiaras were replaced by a jeweled pendant placed on the forehead, Hindu fashion, or by jeweled clips and rhinestone bands as wide as bracelets, sparkling in the hair.[2]

Vintage ads provide clues about how jewelry was worn.

The ad in Figure 2 shows an elegant woman in a hostess coat accessorized with layers of pearls and a multi-strand necklace. A 1949 advertisement shown in Figure 3 reveals a fashionable pairing of shorter pearls with a two strand necklace; the model's wrist is bedecked with a fabulous bracelet and her glove is adjusted accordingly to show the bracelet to its best advantage.

A 1947 ad, for Marvella shows "sixty inches of beautiful simulated pearls...to twist, to twine, to drape!" The pearls are shown as a bracelet, a creatively draped and wrapped necklace, and as a belt (see Figure 4).

Today Is "Joan Crawford Day"

Vintage costume jewelry evokes earlier eras when glamour was de rigueur. Even the already glamorous could feel more so. A 36-year-old Kenneth Jay Lane being interviewed by a writer for the *Saturday Evening Post* once said that "with jewelry you can play any role you like." He

Figure 2. Golden hostess coat vintage advertisement (date unknown).

---

[1] Pinch of War Felt in Novelty Exhibit, *New York Times*, February 5, 1942.

[2] Fashion Jewelry Reflects Yesteryear and the Orient, *New York Times*, November 12, 1953.

Introduction: Today Is "Joan Crawford Day"

Figure 3. Forstmann Woolen Company vintage advertisement from *LIFE* Magazine, April 4, 1949.

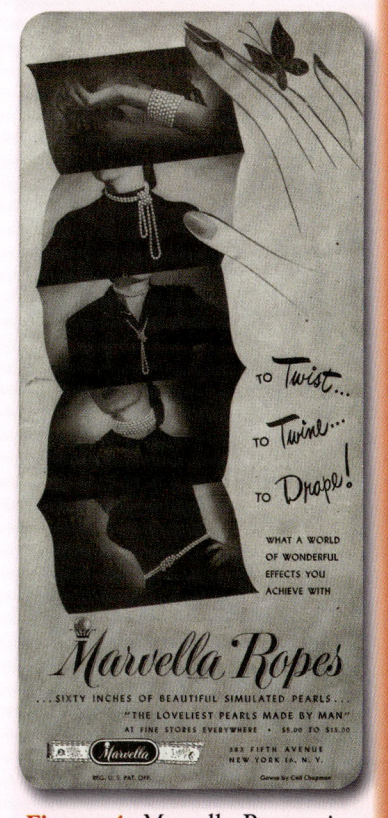

featured in this book. Fortunately these lovely gifts came to me along with their stories. One small, delicate brooch was admired many years ago in a shop window. The admiration lasted for months. Finally the time came when a young woman was able to afford the extravagance. That day she returned to the store and bought herself the coveted pin shown below on the left. I love the sweet nostalgia evoked by such stories. I feel privileged to be a steward of these lovely items whose history I can add to and then someday pass along so that someone, my daughter perhaps, may add yet another precious chapter.

Figure 4. Marvella Ropes vintage advertisement from *Good Housekeeping*.

recounted a time when Greta Garbo visited his Park Avenue showroom where she spent hours "being everyone from Theda Bara to Camille — just with earrings." Try to imagine even plain and unadorned Greta Garbo as anything *but* glamorous. But even she transcended the mundane with the help of a beautiful accessory. The forever lovely Miss Garbo is shown in a photo from *LIFE* magazine in Figure 5.

It is certainly true that an Eisenberg brooch or Hobé bib necklace can make me feel glamorous. It's even better when I know the story behind a piece of jewelry. I was recently given several pieces of vintage costume jewelry, some of which are

Petite and sweet, this pin features green and white enamel accented with a small green stone. It dates to the early 1940s. A young lady once waited months to be able to afford this delicate pin. Unsigned, $20.00 – 30.00.

Figure 5. Glamorous Greta Garbo: used with permission. Evening Standard / Hulton Archive / Getty Images.

11

Introduction: Knowledge Is Power

Knowledge Is Power
(or at least important)

Because I so often wear costume jewelry, I am often asked questions such as, "Where did you get such a lovely pin?" Or, from people who know something about vintage costume jewelry, I might be asked about the piece's designer, where I purchased it, or even what one might expect to pay for such an item. Sometimes I was able to answer the questions and sometimes not. I realized I wanted to learn much more and began my research by looking at the growing collection of information about vintage costume jewelry. I discovered many beautifully photographed and well written books. These books provide hours of reading pleasure about a subject I love. At the same time they are invaluable reference books.

The first book I purchased was entitled *Costume Jewelry: Identification and Values* by Cherri Simonds. I was astounded that some of the pieces in my collection were in her book; two were even on the cover! About the same time I purchased a copy of Lillian Baker's book entitled *Fifty Years of Collectible Fashion Jewelry: 1925 – 1975*. Ms. Baker was serious about providing a reference work for collectors. She had unique first-hand knowledge about Emmons jewelry and the way it was marketed. In 1952 she became a fashion show director for Emmons and soon became a district director. Julia Carroll's *Costume Jewelry 101* and Fred Rezazadeh's *Costume Jewelry* are also excellent sources of information. Every time I read them I learn something new.

I also enjoy the simple pleasure of looking at photographs of jewelry. Among my favorites are *Costume Jewelers, The Golden Age of Design*, by Joanne Dubbs Ball; The *Great Pretenders* by Lyngerda Kelly and Nancy Schiffer; *Rhinestone Jewelry* by Leigh Leshner; and *Costume Jewelry* by Judith Miller. The classic, information-packed and beautifully photographed *Jewels of Fantasy: Costume Jewelry of the 20th Century* by Deanna Ferretti Cera and the Brunialtis' *A Tribute to America: Costume Jewelry, 1935 – 1950*, belong in every serious collector's library. For me, the only thing more fun than collecting costume jewelry is reading about it!

Many websites also feature

Napier gold-tone umbrella pin with clear rhinestone accents. Signed NAPIER on the inside of the umbrella handle. $35.00 – 50.00.

information about various costume jewelry designers and manufacturers. A list of websites that I have found to be very helpful can be found in the bibliography.

The discovery of new information can be as exciting as finally finding a signature. I can recall the careful examination of a brooch shaped like a closed umbrella that was given to me by my aunt. I couldn't understand how this lovely pin was unsigned. While cleaning it, I turned it in a way that revealed a discreet Napier signature on the umbrella handle. The brooch is featured on the bottom left.

Signatures and other markings can be found in obvious places such as on the back of a pin inscribed on a cartouche. Or, they can be found in subtle and clever places that are more difficult to discover. The early work of Marcel Boucher was discreetly marked with a small and highly stylized "MB." It requires a loupe to discover this mark. I have read many stories of collectors who just knew there was a signature or mark lurking somewhere on a piece of their jewelry. They tilted and turned it, looked down on it and up at it. Finally, they found the mark they always knew was there.

Elzac brooch missing the Lucite wings.

It is important to find out as much as possible about the jewelry you collect. Armed with knowledge, you will buy pieces and sets that are intact and not missing important elements. I once purchased an Elzac brooch (shown above) without the Lucite wing. I did not realize it was missing because I was unfamiliar with the original design. The patent for this brooch shows its intended design (see Figure 6).

Look at as many pieces of jewelry as you can; read as much as possible and closely examine photographs. Research primary source documents including old ads, patents, newspaper columns, and jeweler's buyers guides to learn all you can about original designs. The archives of *Women's Wear Daily* are also available for a fee. From original sources, reference books, and online websites, one can learn much about the intended designs of selected manufacturers and designers. Collectors should also join the Vintage Fashion and Costume Jewelry (VFCJ) organization.

Introduction: What to Buy

Figure 6. Patent for Elzac brooch.

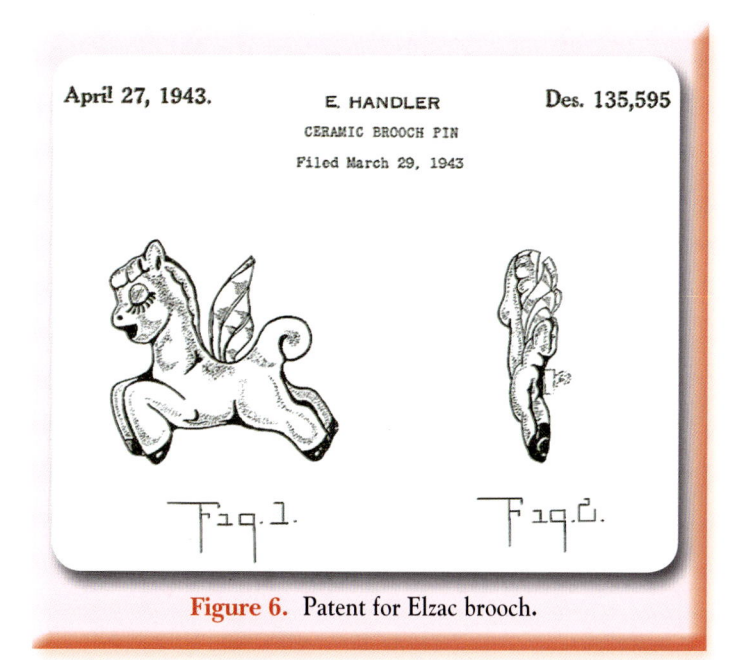

VFCJ publishes an excellent quarterly magazine which is full of constantly updated information about the field.[3]

No one can beat the diligence of Pat Seal[4] for dedicated research. Following her intuition, she discovered that Leo Glass jewelry was made during the 1930s contrary to reference books that stated he began his business in the early 1940s. How? By looking through every issue of *Vogue* and *Harper's Bazaar* that was available to her. Over a four year period, for at least eight hours at a time, she would look through magazines spanning the years 1901 to 1979!

Costume Jewelry's Ups, Downs, and Ups

Despite its strong showing throughout much of the twentieth century, interest in costume jewelry faded in the 1970s. The decline was so dramatic that many companies had to shut their doors, among them the giant Coro.

Even the auction of Joan Crawford's jewelry in 1978 did not attract the attention her collection deserved. Ms. Crawford was an avid collector of Joseff and Miriam Haskell jewelry among other designers and was often photographed wearing pieces from her fabulous costume jewelry collection. High profile bidders like Andy Warhol could not stir up much interest in the auction.

Just a few short years later, costume jewelry would make a dramatic come-back. Ironically, its resurgence was aided by several high-profile auctions. During the 1980s fabulous private collections became available to collectors and were met with amazing results. A decade after the Crawford auction, prospective bidders would encircle a New York City block to wait in line for the auction of the private collections of Andy Warhol including his famous Bakelite collection. Sotheby's auction of Diana Vreeland's collection of 1950 – 1960s costume jewelry garnered much attention and included pieces by Yves Saint Laurent, Chanel, and Kenneth Jay Lane, among others. Sotheby's auction of the Duchess of Windsor's gem collection created quite a stir. The Franklin Mint, Carolee, Harrods, Eximious of London, Kenneth Jay Lane, Adrienne, and Butler and Wilson made their own versions of some of the pieces sold at the Sotheby's auction. Carolee copied the Duchess's flamingo pin and they sold quickly. Evidently, the Duchess loved that pin as there are many photographs of her wearing the original. I was fortunate to find a Carolee brooch (shown below) but not of the famous flamingo. The pin I bought was not copied from a piece of jewelry in the Sotheby's auction catalog; however it reads "Duchess's Royal Navy." Costume reproductions of the Duchess' jewelry continue to be popular today and consistently command high prices.

Trifari further livened up the costume jewelry scene by releasing a collection of jewelry based upon their 1945 – 1970 archives, including their popular jelly belly brooches. Costume jewelry was back. Boy was it back!

Antiqued silver-tone brooch with green and navy blue enameled accents and clear rhinestone trim. It reads "Duchess Royal Navy" and is signed CAROLEE© on an oval cartouche. Carolee was one of many who successfully copied selected items from the jewelry collection of the Duchess of Windsor. $75.00 – 100.00.

What to Buy

It's pretty simple. Buy what you like. My own collection reflects my eclectic taste. No matter what trends dictate, purchase jewelry that you will enjoy wearing, handling, looking at, and taking care of. If you only buy what is

---
[3] VFCJ, P.O. Box 265, Glen Oaks, NY 11004 (e:mail: VFCJ@aol.com)
[4] Treasures from Yesterday Vintage Jewelry

Introduction: What to Buy

trendy, you will pay premium prices. Right now Juliana-style jewelry is very sought after by collectors. When that happens, the prices go up. In the early 1980s, I purchased a few Juliana brooches with matching earrings for a fraction of current prices.

Many collectors appreciate the fine workmanship of jewelry signed HAR, the exotic countenances featured in Selro and Selini pieces, the whimsical Hattie Carnegie critters, or Elzac's Victim of Fashion collages. Others may prefer a more classic look such as a traditional Eisenberg clip or Trifari rhinestone brooch. Still others dig a little deeper to find interesting pieces. In the first volume of *Inside the Jewelry Box*, Ann Mitchell Pitman focuses attention on companies that have had limited exposure in other books, including Claudette, Calvaire, and Les Bernard. If you are very fortunate, you will be able to add family pieces to your collection as I have done.

There is something for everyone. And there is plenty of it. If you buy what you like, your collection will provide you with years of pleasure. I even buy what I like as gifts for friends. Luckily they enjoy vintage costume jewelry as much as I do. Last year, I found a bin of Lucite earrings at an antique market. I scooped up several pairs to tuck into gifts. What fun!

Condition, Condition, Condition

Except in rare cases, condition is paramount. Collectors must consider condition when deciding whether to purchase an item. Vintage costume jewelry is delicate and fragile under the best conditions. Even careful handling can provoke a disaster. I have actually damaged pieces that I just purchased when unwrapping them at home! I once lost the pearl face of a figural brooch just a few short hours after purchasing the item. While unwrapping the pin to show my husband, the pearl fell out; we searched on hand and foot and could not find that pearl! The photo below shows the pin with a (now) replaced pearl face. Even with cautious handling stones can fall out.

Head mounted magnifier which leaves my hands free to work on jewelry.

While sorting through my jewelry, I discovered a missing stone in a pair of rhinestone earrings that I know were perfect at one time. Perhaps I lost it while wearing the earrings and didn't realize it. Fortunately this type of problem is easy to fix. Serious collectors must be prepared to undertake straightforward repairs and should keep on hand a properly equipped tool box.

I have a large plastic tool kit outfitted with glue, non-abrasive cleaners, cotton swabs, needle nose pliers, tweezers, and wooden toothpicks. I also have a dental pick for helping dislodge stones from jewelry items that are beyond repair. I use a head mounted magnifier which leaves my hands free to work. It is made by Optivisor and is a precision binocular headband magnifier. It provides unrestricted efficiency, reduces eye strain, and leaves hands free.[5] (See above photo.) I think the best source of repair stones is vintage jewelry that can't be fixed and earrings that have no mate. I have a Kramer earring whose mate I lost when I wore them. I have taken clear rhinestones from the remaining earring to replace stones in several brooches. I also keep a supply of jewelry pieces in my tool kit. I leave the stones in their fittings until they are needed because they can be lost so easily. I have even misplaced tiny stones in the midst of a repair! For more complex repairs, I usually contact an expert such as MRStones. Matthew and Patricia Ribarich can provide vintage stones that match the quality of the stones that need to be replaced and they can set them for you as well.[6]

Replacing missing stones is one thing. But there are

A rootin' tootin' cowgirl with replacement pearl face. The original pearl is somewhere in my house! Measuring a petite 1", this pin was probably one of a pair of scatter pins. The cowgirl has just drawn her gun and is about ready to start shooting. Note the tiny blue rhinestones on her sleeves and along the hemline of her dress. $15.00 – 20.00.

[5] http://www.doneganoptical.com/optivisor
[6] See www.MRstones.com

Introduction: Buying on eBay

other types of damage that cannot be repaired easily. The best thing is to be careful when you are shopping but this is easier said than done. Even though I've been collecting for many years, I still get excited by a display of jewelry in an antique shop. I think the beauty of vintage costume jewelry, particularly rhinestones, is amplified when many pieces are grouped together. Then a few pieces will invariably grab my attention. My advice? Leave the decision about whether to buy until after you have thoroughly examined any piece in which you are interested. Try to avoid the disappointment of paying too much for a piece of repaired jewelry or a set that's not really a set at all.

To examine potential purchases, I carry both a magnifying glass and a loupe. When my daughter is with me, she helps me examine items carefully. She will caution me about loose or missing stones or other damage. And sometimes we both miss flaws! Be sure the light is sufficient to clearly examine jewelry. You may even consider carrying a small flashlight. Antique shops and indoor flea markets are not always well illuminated and not everyone will let you walk outside with a piece of jewelry to examine it. Most damage is extremely difficult to detect without magnification or adequate light. I recently discovered an ornate Egyptian revival necklace and bracelet that was very beautifully made and very old. I looked it over and decided to examine it more closely; I was quickly deciding that I would buy it. When I examined the pieces with brighter light, I saw pervasive green corrosion throughout the metal. The set went back into the display case.

Another time I wasn't so prudent. I spotted a striking enamel and glass bug brooch. This bright orange beauty caught my eye as it stood out among the other pieces in the display case. I bought the brooch without examining it closely. When I later examined the piece, I found it was missing an antenna! (See photo below.) It was a bitter lesson for which I could only blame my own impetuousness. Unfortunately, all collectors share similar stories.

Reputable dealers will usually allow you to examine pieces with some type of magnifier and may even provide you with one. Be on the lookout for broken metal, significant metal wear, or

The beautiful orange color is what attracted my eye to this fly pin. The glass body and beautifully enameled wings with orange rhinestone head make this a spectacular brooch. Unfortunately, it is missing one of its antennae. The extent of the damage is such that it is difficult to assign a value to this piece. It is signed under the right wing Original by Robert© on a cartouche shaped like a palette.

metal loss due to corrosion. These types of damage cannot be repaired without significant investment. Even then it is not always possible and the repair may considerably reduce the value of the item.

Buying on eBay

When I first began collecting, I bought from antique shops, flea markets, and my local church's yard sales. I found many lovely items this way. Now the quantity and variety of designer pieces available on eBay and online dealers is simply staggering. Among my favorites is HAR. Their small, whimsical creatures, elegant Blackamoors, Asian figures, cobra, dragon, and fortune teller pieces appear regularly on eBay. It would take years of looking through antique shops to come up with what one can find online in a matter of weeks or months.

Buying on eBay presents both opportunities and challenges, because of the quantity and variety of items offered prices can be very competitive. Conversely, the number of collectors who buy on eBay can really drive up prices on certain highly collectible pieces. A downside is that collectors cannot carefully examine items, hold them to feel their weight, look closely for metal wear or loss, or detect loose or missing stones as one can in an antique shop or flea market. The buyer must rely on the seller's description and photographs. Of course you can always ask questions and request more photographs; this can be very helpful. It is also important to check sellers' feedback as well as their selling/return policies. Reputable eBay sellers place a high value on their feedback ratings and will make every effort to satisfy their customers. I once won an auction for a large and stunning brooch loaded with green and clear rhinestones and peach-colored opaque cabochons. When the item arrived, I joyfully examined my new purchase using a loupe. You can imagine my disappointment when I found significant metal loss tucked under the cabochons. I contacted the seller immediately who was surprised to hear of the problem. The metal loss was extremely difficult to detect but it was there. Fortunately I was able to return the item for a full refund. In general, my recommendation for eBay buyers is to identify favorite sellers whose items are consistent with their descriptions. Then buy with confidence.

EBay selling prices now help determine current estimated values. *Vintage Fashion and Costume Jewelry* magazine features a column entitled "eBay Closings Since the Last Issue" to regularly document current selling prices and provide a way for collectors to keep track of the market. Since location also plays a part in determining values, the magazine has another column that features prices based on authors' buying trips around the country. What sells for a premium in New York City will sell for less or more in another location.

Introduction: Fakes and Copies

Fakes and Copies

Fakes are sold everywhere. I have seen rhinestone brooches marked "Weiss" appear with surprising regularity on eBay. Several of the same designs are even being auctioned at the same time! A recent *New York Times* article describes several instances of buyers who bought jewelry lots on eBay and later found out the pieces were fakes.[7]

Keep in mind that many signed and unsigned pieces of jewelry were deliberately made to resemble signed pieces. In 1937 Napier created their own version of Schiaparelli's globe-encircling charm bracelet. Napier also created versions of other Schiaparelli jewelry as well as pieces made by Chanel. CRAFT made a copy of a famous CORO brooch depicting the singer Josephine Baker (see photo on left). The original CORO brooch was featured in the Jewels of Fantasy exhibition. The design of the pin matches design patent 133,741 issued on September 8, 1942, to A. Katz (Figure 7). These and other copies were made to intentionally imitate favored pieces made by competitors. This jewelry is not only vintage it is very collectible. The pieces are signed by the maker so that collectors are not fooled. Contemporary fakes are marked so as to intentionally deceive buyers. Fake Weiss brooches are signed WEISS; the Josephine Baker brooch is signed CRAFT.

Fakes can even drive down the prices of authentic pieces. Whereas a vintage Weiss brooch could sell for as much as $150.00, the profusion of copies and counterfeits is discouraging to collectors and makes potential buyers wary.

I have seen on eBay what appeared to be the famous HAR full figure Asian figural brooch. The seller noted in her description that while the brooch looked like the famous HAR piece, it was not, nor was it made by ART,

A large brooch possibly depicting the singer and dancer Josephine Baker. However, this brooch is signed CRAFT and was made by the Verris. Interestingly, Gene Verri worked for CORO from 1933 to 1966. The Verris are using their company name so as not to confuse collectors who will know, because of the CRAFT mark, that this is a newer brooch.

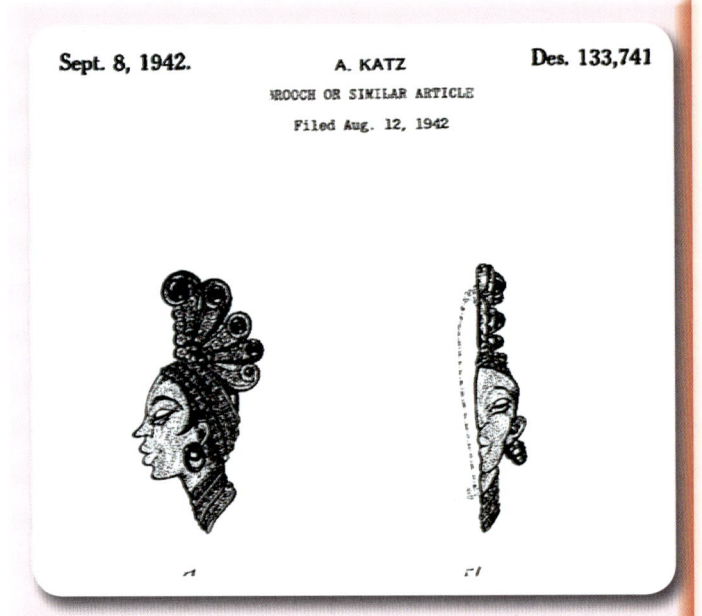

Figure 7. Copy of A. Katz patent for brooch or similar article.

which marketed similar figures. In fact the piece was marked "Made in China" in an oval cartouche on the back of the brooch. Unfortunately not all reproductions are marked like this brooch. It is up to the buyer to ask questions, inspect and examine, and walk away when in doubt. A simple rule to follow is "when prices go up, the fakes come out." Selected pieces by Trifari, Eisenberg, Staret, Weiss, Lisner, and others have all been copied.

Sometimes dealers can unwittingly sell fakes especially if costume jewelry is not their area of expertise. Novice collectors should avoid buying expensive pieces until they acquire more knowledge and familiarity with vintage jewelry. Sometimes even more experienced collectors can have difficulty discerning fakes from the real thing. Eisenberg fakes flooded the market in the 1980s. They were gold-plated pieces with colored rhinestones and were reportedly difficult to detect even by more experienced collectors. Even the experts can be duped.

An excellent way to build a collection is to purchase from reputable dealers who provide an assortment of authentic vintage items. Once you develop a relationship they will also be on the lookout for jewelry they know you collect. There are several online dealers from whom I have purchased many beautiful and high quality items. I have included a list of my favorites in the bibliography. Reliable dealers are helpful and knowledgeable; many are vintage jewelry collectors themselves. Others specialize in selected manufacturers and designers. For those on a budget, some dealers will offer flexible payment options which can help you afford more rare and fabulous items. No matter where you decide to buy, the bottom line is — know the seller.

[7] Hafner, Katie. Seeing Fakes, Angry Traders Confront eBay. *New York Times*, January 29, 2006.

Introduction: Children as Collectors

It Costs How Much?

Various factors affect current prices of vintage costume jewelry. Values change with changing tastes. Fortunately many of the most popular and informative jewelry value and identification guides are updated regularly to reflect this fluid market. The aspects that affect value are straightforward. Complete sets command higher prices than individual pieces because they are harder to find. Original boxes or jewelry with original tags further increase the value of items. Original packaging and/or complete sets can increase prices by an average of 30% or more. So desirable are complete sets that some collectors will only purchase them and not individual pieces. While signatures help a collector identify the jewelry's creators, many wonderful items were not signed, including selected pieces by Weiss, Schreiner, and Eisenberg. Kenneth Jay Lane once recounted a story about jewelry that escaped his workroom without signatures. Even with the utmost care, pieces slipped by now and then, he said. Clients could bring back the jewelry and get a letter signed by Mr. Lane indicating the item was his.

While signed pieces are easy to catalog, many unsigned pieces can be identified by looking for certain style characteristics. Materials used, quality of construction, and other telltale clues can point to a particular maker. Some Eisenberg, Weiss, early Miriam Haskell pieces, and Juliana style jewelry were unsigned. Increasing your knowledge about design clues will increase your chances of identifying and purchasing fabulous items for considerably less than the cost of signed pieces.

There Are Still Bargains

The days of 25¢ brooches may be gone but there are still bargains. I recently purchased a retro modern style sterling brooch signed "Brookraft" at a flea market. It was sitting on a vendor's table among many other non-jewelry items and made a poor showing because it was very soiled. For dollars the brooch was on its way home with me. As I polished it with a cotton swab and nonabrasive cleaner, the pin revealed its beauty (see photo bottom left).

I once purchased a pair of Eisenberg rhinestone chandelier earrings. While stopping by one of my favorite antique markets I spotted the earrings. I was in a hurry so I quickly checked for loose or missing stones and scanned the backs. All seemed well so I purchased the earrings for eight dollars. I later discovered an "E" in script on the earring backs! The letter "E" in block or script, without the copyright symbol, appeared on Eisenberg jewelry between 1942 – 1945. What an exciting find!

As hard as it is for me to believe, not everyone is interested in costume jewelry. However I have found that most dealers will feature at least a few pieces, testament to the current interest among buyers. A dealer's passion may be Roseville or old postcards. In these cases, their pieces may be priced lower than they might be by someone who sells only jewelry.

Children as Collectors

My daughter began her collecting quite casually. She accompanied me into a local antique shop where I browsed for awhile. She usually headed for the candy bowl and a chair, but on this occasion she browsed with me. She found a small blue and white butterfly pin and asked me to purchase it for her (photo on top of next page, center pin). When we arrived home, we found a small container with compartments that she could use to store her new pin. After that, she needed no encouragement to accompany me. Her small collection began to grow and she learned much about the items she now collects. She uses a loupe and magnifing glass and helps me inspect potential purchases. While shopping, we examine items together and I point out signatures and other interesting aspects. She has became proficient at finding loose or missing stones, worn fittings, metal wear, and verdigris. We assembled a small tool kit as we learned together how to care for our jewelry. Collecting vintage costume jewelry has captured and held her interest.

We sit together for hours, sorting through our jewelry to clean, inspect, and learn. These peaceful moments are rare in our hectic and overscheduled lives. When we are at odds about homework or chores we can always agree on the beauty of a newly acquired piece of jewelry. Our hobby is neutral ground for my preteen daughter and me and provides us with a place apart from daily demands. The simple act of cleaning a new treasure is an experience that is both restorative and calming.

Retro style brooch with curled metal and a large emerald cut center aquamarine typically seen in this type of jewelry. The brooch measures 3" across. It is signed BROOKRAFT on an oval cartouche. $75.00 – 100.00.

Introduction: Children as Collectors

Lower Left: Silver-tone filigree moth with plenty of detail. This looks like sterling but we couldn't find a mark anywhere. Unsigned. $15.00 – 20.00. Middle: Petite blue and white enameled butterfly pin. This was my daughter's first pin. She liked the color and shape of this. It measures just 1" x 1" and is unsigned. $10.00 – 15.00. Upper Right: Lightweight and colorful butterfly pin. This is not a vintage pin but we liked it anyway. Unsigned. $5.00 – 10.00.

I learned firsthand the value of a hobby for children. I can recall accompanying my parents on their buying trips. They collected pottery and to be included in their adventures was a privilege; to be allowed to wander through shops taught me restraint and self-control. My parents trusted me to look and not touch. They took the time to teach me about differentiating factors such as quality, identification marks, and condition. As my awareness increased, so did my confidence. I was acquiring knowledge, as my daughter is, that one could never acquire in the course of an average school day. These precious memories taught me that learning can be a joyful and lifelong process.

For my daughter, collecting vintage costume jewelry is also fun. She enjoys dressing up and wearing her pieces on special occasions. That vintage costume jewelry is tangible proof of how history, culture, and art intersect is perhaps of less importance to her. For her first school dance, however, I bought her a pair of open-toe wedge shoes reminiscent of a 1940s style. Because she has learned so much about the necessary style of costume jewelry made during World War II, she had a reference point for her new shoes, a contemporary style with roots in another time.

Caring for Your Collection

Direct sunlight, temperature extremes, and moisture are the enemies of costume jewelry and should be avoided. Moisture is an anathema to foil-backed rhinestones and can damage them irreparably. It causes foil backs to separate from stones.

Excessive handling of jewelry should be avoided; pin backs, clasps, and other fittings should be treated gently and with care. Remember, even "newer" jewelry is decades old!

Your jewelry should be cleaned regularly and especially when you first purchase it. Many times, this will be the item's first cleaning in years. I use a gentle, nonacidic and nonabrasive cleaner that does not contain alcohol or ammonia. I don't spray the cleaner directly onto the jewelry because it is impossible to control where the moisture goes. Rather, I put a few drops of cleaner on a cotton swab and gently rub it over the jewelry surface. I also use plastic needle-nose pliers for working a small, tight wad of saturated cotton into hard-to-clean spots on the back of intricate pieces like clamper bracelets. This must be done carefully to avoid scratching the metal or stones.

Accumulations of soil can often be found on jewelry where it touched the skin. This includes earring backs, the underside of bracelets, and necklaces including clasps and the length that would lay on the wearer's neck. Over time jewelry can be compromised if not cleaned properly. The collected residue may be from make-up, body creams, dusting powder, or hair products. Any residue should be cleaned off as soon as possible after you purchase jewelry. Likewise, when you anticipate wearing a piece of jewelry from your collection, skip the cosmetics and skin creams in places where your jewelry will come into contact with your skin. The photo of the pearls on the top of the next page reveals that where the pearls once lay upon the wearer's neck, the nacre has deteriorated.

If left untended, accumulated soil can lead to verdigris. I have read that catsup, lemon juice, or vinegar can be useful for removing it. However, none of the suggestions are a panacea. The presence of even a small amount of verdigris is evidence the metal has been compromised. By cleaning your jewelry all you can hope to do is stem the progression of metal loss. Even though we have all done it, I would recommend not purchasing jewelry with verdigris. If you already have a favorite or family piece that is compromised, clean it as best you can and store it separately from your other treasures.

Regular cleanings, careful handling, and dry, roomy storage will keep your costume jewelry safe and free from damage for many years.

Where these well worn pearls rested on the wearer's neck, the nacre has deteriorated.

Fashion and Jewelry Timeline

Excavations of ancient civilizations reveal secrets about the mores and manners of generations past. Archeologists uncovered pots, hunting implements, and…jewelry. Available materials were fashioned into accents that were at once artistic, imaginative, and beautiful. So enduring are some of the designs that they continue to serve as inspiration today.

During the twentieth century, modern manufacturing methods were born. We made planes and trains, automobiles and computers, and some of the most beautiful costume jewelry ever designed. The foundation was laid in the late nineteenth century. In 1875 Napier began production in North Attleboro, Massachusetts, under the name Whitney & Rice. It was the first company of its kind, producing non-precious jewelry along with giftware and silver novelties. A year later Whiting and Davis established their reputation by designing and producing beautiful, finely woven gold and silver mesh bags. Later they would add distinctive jewelry to their line.

In 1892, Daniel Swarovski patented a design for a machine that could cut gemstones with perfect precision. He perfected the grinding and polishing of hundreds of paste stones in one process.

By 1900, it was generally accepted that jewelry could be an art form in its own right and not simply a fashion accessory. Jewelry was valued for its design and workmanship.

At the coronation of her husband, King Edward

Fashion and Jewelry Timeline

VII, Queen Alexandra initiated the fad for narrow pearl chokers. She layered pearls and diamonds and dazzled onlookers: she wore five diamond chokers and seven strings of magnificent pearls!

A few years later, Bakelite was developed, the first fully synthetic plastic. It wasn't until 1927, however, when the Catalin Corporation acquired the patent for Bakelite that jewelry making with this material would begin in earnest.

Popular jewelry colors were influenced by current events. Suffragettes wore purple, white, and green representing loyalty, purity, and hope. The suffragette newspaper, *Votes for Women* had a regular feature called "Concerning Dress" which focused on fashion. It published a list of businesses that provided garments and accessories in the suffragette colors.

In 1914, Eisenberg was founded in Chicago as a manufacturer of off-the-rack but upscale clothing. Later they would commission colorless paste clips and brooches as accents for their ready-to-wear line. The clips and brooches could not be purchased separately but proved so popular that shoppers started helping themselves. The result — Eisenberg started its own line of costume jewelry.

By 1920, jewelry was becoming more stylized and two-dimensional as the transition to Art Deco began. The bandeaux, plumed aigrettes, long tasseled neck chains, and pendulous earrings actually became established before World War 1, even though these are typically associated with the 1920s.

Practicality took over with the onset of the first World War. Elaborate hairstyles no longer seemed appropriate, so many women cut their hair short. Many joined the workforce. Women who joined the armed forces wore uniforms and had a considerable impact on everyday fashions.

In the early 1920s flappers wore drop-waisted dresses decorated with pearls, crystals, and tiny mirrors. The cover of *Vogue* in 1924 showed the fashion for costume jewelry: beads were worn long and sometimes knotted; the jewelry ensemble might include a choker, dangling earrings, a matching pin, and bracelet. Long strings of beads or pearls suited the flat-fronted dresses. Haircuts continued to be short and boyish and earrings were worn long.

Probably the most influential designer of the 1920s was Coco Chanel. Her cardigan suits, sailor jackets, pullovers, and trousers were extremely popular. Costume jewelry was presented as an important part of her outfits. Chanel induced women to spend small fortunes on artificial pearls. Jewelry that was frankly and obviously fake, with impossibly huge sizes and colors, became Chanel's trademark.

Even with its Parisian roots and European designers, the costume jewelry phenomena was distinctly American. The United States was foremost in the manufacture of costume jewelry with its magnificent tools, choice of materials, and perfected factory facilities. It was a profitable business; the costume jewelry industry was making millions of dollars. Several cities in Massachusetts had achieved distinction as centers of costume jewelry. Huge plants were employing as many as 400 people. World-wide, the largest of these was in Providence, Rhode Island. During the 1920s and 1930s many of the greatest costume jewelry firms were established or experienced phenomenal growth.

At the same time, close to 75% of the stones that were being used were imported. Italy was making mosaics; Japan was making pearls; Czechoslovakia and Austria were making glass; and from France came style. Russian antique effects showed up as the Soviets displayed the Czar's jewels. Color was the basic fashion factor.

After the first World War, costume jewelry came on the scene full force. The aim was to endow every woman with glamour. Jewels were designed as attention getters and conversation pieces. Jewelry was being sold everywhere. Woolworth's featured jewelry that was fashionable and affordable (see Figure 8). By 1925, plastics and costume jewelry achieved distinction at the 1925 Exhibition in Paris.

Contemporary events influenced jewelry designs. After the discovery of King Tutankhamen's tomb in Egypt, oriental fashions took hold with a particular fascination for all things Egyptian. A passion for Egyptian designs would be seen again and again throughout the twentieth century as moviegoers watched Greta Garbo, Claudette Colbert, Vivian Leigh, and Elizabeth Taylor play Cleopatra (see Figure 9).

The influence of famous people could also be seen in jewelry designs. The young Josephine Baker's scant costumes, elaborate headdresses, and provocative cabaret routines are legendary. For years, her likeness was depicted in many jewelry designs which included details of the fabulous costumes she wore during her performances. In particular, Chanel and Coro brooches depicting Josephine Baker are coveted, extremely rare, and sought after by collectors (See Figure 10).

By the end of the 1920s, attitudes toward jewelry again changed. Jewelry became a focal point on the costume rather than to just complement the body. Neck chains and aigrettes went out of style and compact earrings replaced pendant earrings. New jewelry styles affixed to the dress

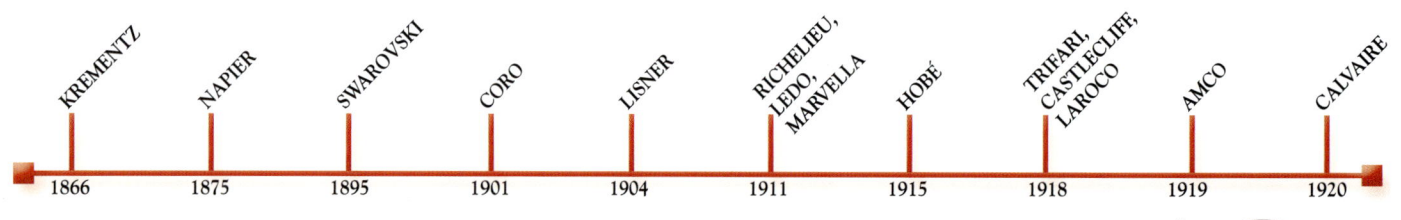

KREMENTZ	NAPIER	SWAROVSKI	CORO	LISNER	RICHELIEU, LEDO, MARVELLA	HOBÉ	TRIFARI, CASTLECLIFF, LAROCO	AMCO	CALVAIRE
1866	1875	1895	1901	1904	1911	1915	1918	1919	1920

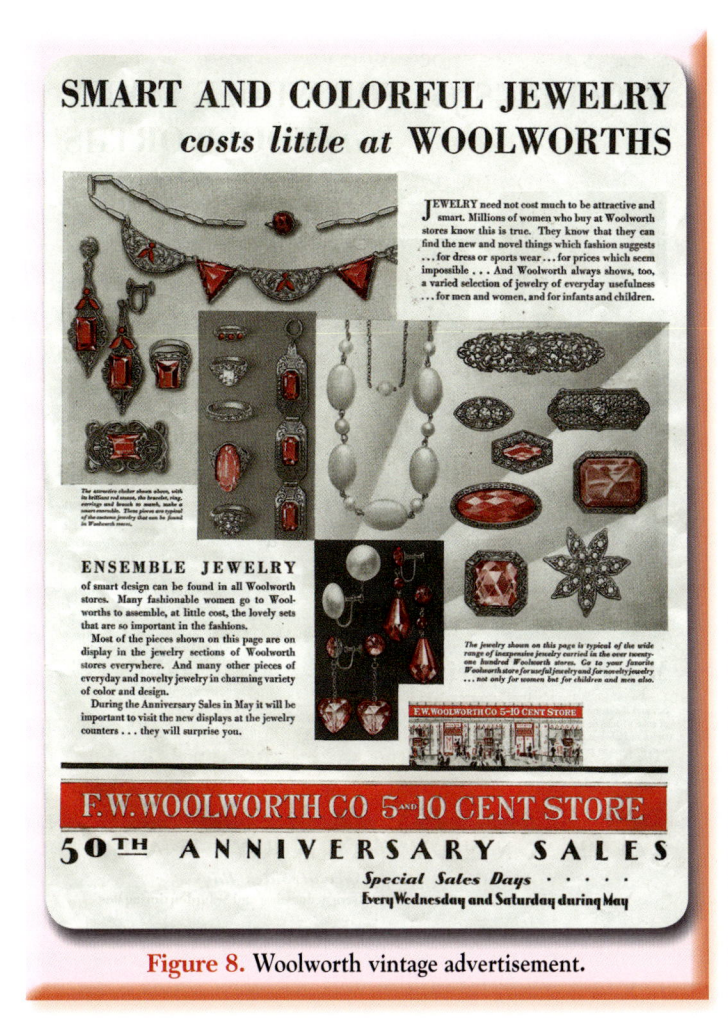

Fashion and Jewelry Timeline

Figure 8. Woolworth vintage advertisement.

shields, and crowns. A new scarf clip/pin was shown at the New York accessories show.

It was the age of the gadget. Clips were made in pairs so the two could be united in a double clip brooch or even a bracelet. Clips were everywhere and used for all occasions; they ranged from hand-carved woods in animal designs to the more extravagant Schiaparelli jeweled clips. They became one of the most popular and versatile forms of adornment ever.

A new type of choker necklace was also introduced which was often made of flat disks cut in various shapes. They were called bib necklaces. Mother-of-pearl was an extremely popular material for these necklaces. They were made of very large flat leaves or flowers that were about 4" wide in front and narrowed to almost nothing toward the nape.

By 1937, department stores had doubled the space rather than the person and included clips which clamped to necklines or lapels.

As the new decade began, women were wearing more variety and color than ever before. Jewels were worn everywhere and for all occasions. Practical cork or wood beads with bathing suits were being shown on the fashion pages of the *New York Times*. Elsa Schiaparelli was the most outrageous designer of the 1930s. She often worked with artists including Salvador Dali and Jean Cocteau, and was inventive down to the last detail. She made buttons and jewelry shaped like circus acrobats, guitars, feathers, and lollipops. In the mid-1930s coronation influences were reflected in costume jewelry and included castles, coats-of-arms,

Figure 9. Elizabeth Taylor as Cleopatra: used with permission. Keystone Features / Hulton Archive / Getty Images.

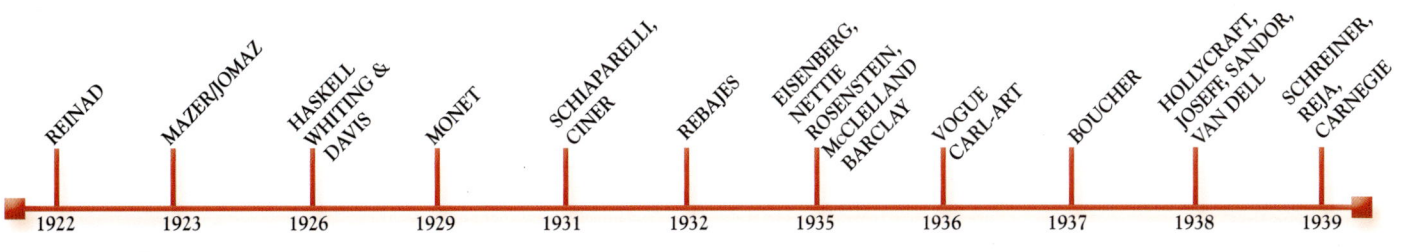

Year	Designer/Brand
1922	REINAD
1923	MAZER/JOMAZ
1926	HASKELL, WHITING & DAVIS
1929	MONET
1931	SCHIAPARELLI, CINER
1932	REBAJES
1935	EISENBERG, NETTIE ROSENSTEIN, McCLELLAND BARCLAY
1936	VOGUE, CARL-ART
1937	BOUCHER
1938	HOLLYCRAFT, JOSEFF, SANDOR, VAN DELL
1939	SCHREINER, REJA, CARNEGIE

Fashion and Jewelry Timeline

Figure 10. Josephine Baker in costume: used with permission. Hulton Archive / Hulton Archive / Getty Images.

allocated to costume jewelry.

Small and discreet jewelry was replaced by overly ornamental costume "junk," a term coined by Schiaparelli. The fashion was to stack several sparkling bracelets on each arm.

Big and "barbaric" trinkets were popular including Egyptian pyramids and Arabian crystals. Chunky jewelry in geometric shapes showed the influence of Art Deco. Lucite was being used with other materials, including wood, in the construction of costume jewelry.

Also in 1937, Marcel Boucher left Cartier to set up his own firm. His first collection of three-dimensional birds was made with colored rhinestones and unusual translucent enamels. They were an instant hit.

Movies were the main form of entertainment and Hollywood led the styles. Evening wear was very sophisticated and glamorous reflecting the style of Jean Harlowe and Carol Lombard among many others. Long strands of beads continued in popularity but were worn slung over the back. Small studs and clips replaced long dangly earrings. So influential was Hollywood that if an actress wore a certain evening gown in a movie, it could cause a stampede at Macy's. They once sold 500,000 copies of an evening gown worn by Joan Crawford. By the time World War II broke out in 1939, the silver screen was firmly established as the place for glamour and escapism. Beautiful and charismatic, movie stars were being used to sell everything from coats to cigarettes.

By 1940 there were only a few diehards who still thought costume jewelry was junk. Costume jewelry's imaginative designs and combinations of every day materials were popular in their own right.

During World War II, classically tailored suits became fashionable. Skirts became shorter, shoulders more square, trousers slimmer, and shoes more sturdy. The suits were ideal for large brooches that were being worn by working women. Large pieces of costume jewelry were the norm. Huge earrings, almost as big around as a quarter and with high settings to make them stand out conspicuously on the ear lobes, were popular. Large brooches featuring pearls, glass stones, and loops of metal ribbon were worn high and wide on the shoulder in line with the collar bone. Typically classic designs can be seen in advertisements of women's clothing during this time (see Figure 11).

Pragmatism drove style. Women were conserving and using what they had. In 1943, *Vogue* magazine featured a dress by American designer Count Rene Willaumez that looked as if it had been made by sewing together scarves. Readers were encouraged to copy the effect by sewing together their own scarves. The magazine also provided patterns for 10 different items of clothing that could be made from a pre-war evening dress.

Ironically, costume jewelry was selling better than ever. The biggest economic gains over the late 1930s were shown by houses marketing costume jewelry. Early American, patriotic, and South American themes were successful in the 1940s "selling picture."

The war dominated the early part of the decade. For

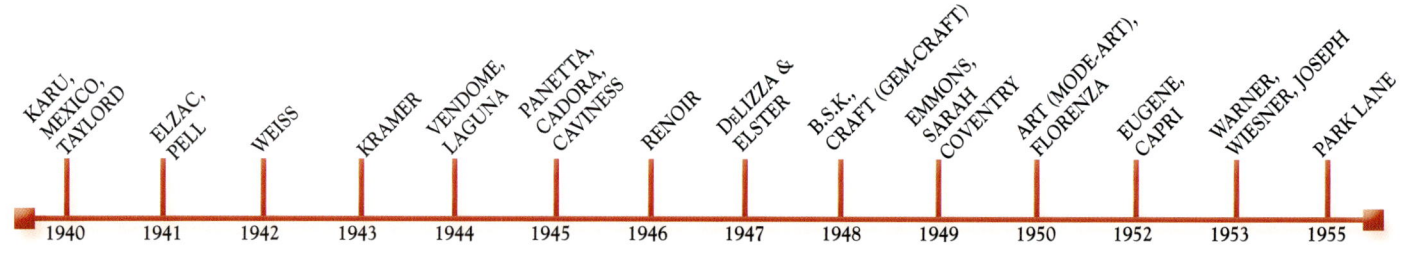

Year	Entry
1940	KARU, MEXICO, TAYLOR
1941	ELZAC, PELL
1942	WEISS
1943	KRAMER
1944	VENDOME, LAGUNA
1945	PANETTA, CADORA, CAVINESS
1946	RENOIR
1947	DeLIZZA & ELSTER
1948	B.S.K., CRAFT (GEM-CRAFT)
1949	EMMONS, SARAH COVENTRY
1950	ART (MODE-ART), FLORENZA
1952	EUGENE, CAPRI
1953	WARNER, WIESNER, JOSEPH
1955	PARK LANE

22

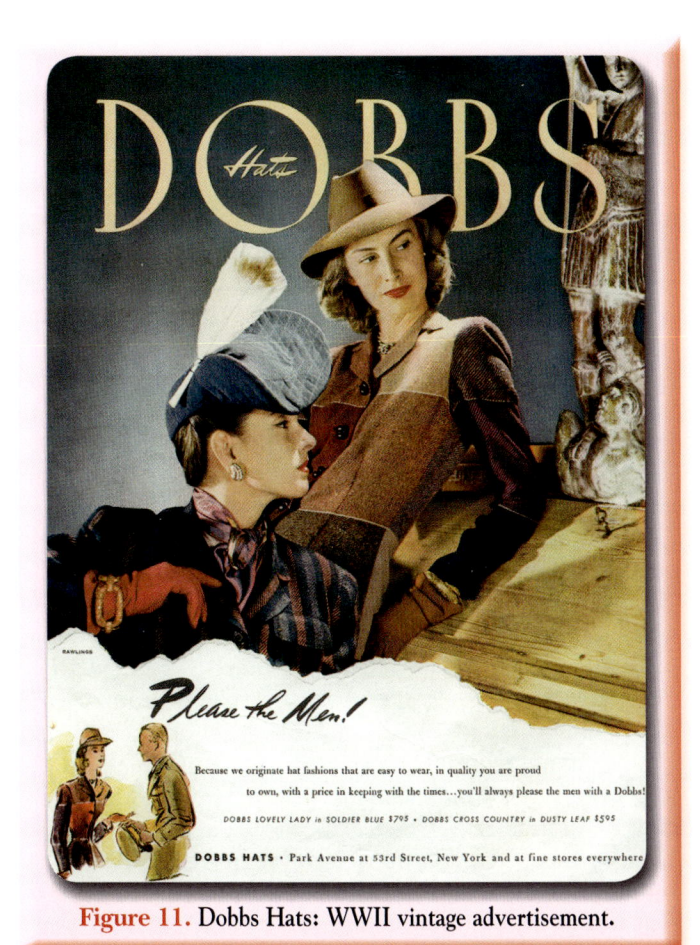

Fashion and Jewelry Timeline

Figure 11. Dobbs Hats: WWII vintage advertisement.

expressly forbidden by a government order. The rhodium was needed to coat reflectors in anti-aircraft search lights. Adapting to the loss during 1944 – 1945, Trifari made its sterling crown brooches; these are among some of their most popular designs ever.

Manufacturers expanded their lines to counteract the metals situation. Jewelry manufacturers and designers began experimenting successfully with alternate materials including plastics and wood. Elzac jewelry employed a variety of ceramic and plastics, feathers and felt.

New plastics were important substitutes for materials formerly used and unavailable because of the elimination of foreign resources. Trifari "jelly bellies" became wildly popular and were created using large polished mounds of Lucite and sterling silver. Brooch designs included poodles, fish, birds, bees, penguins, lizards, and flowers. A few years later Coro made their own versions featuring clear rhinestones in gold-tone metal (see Figure 12). The design patent for the Coro brooches is featured in Figure 13.

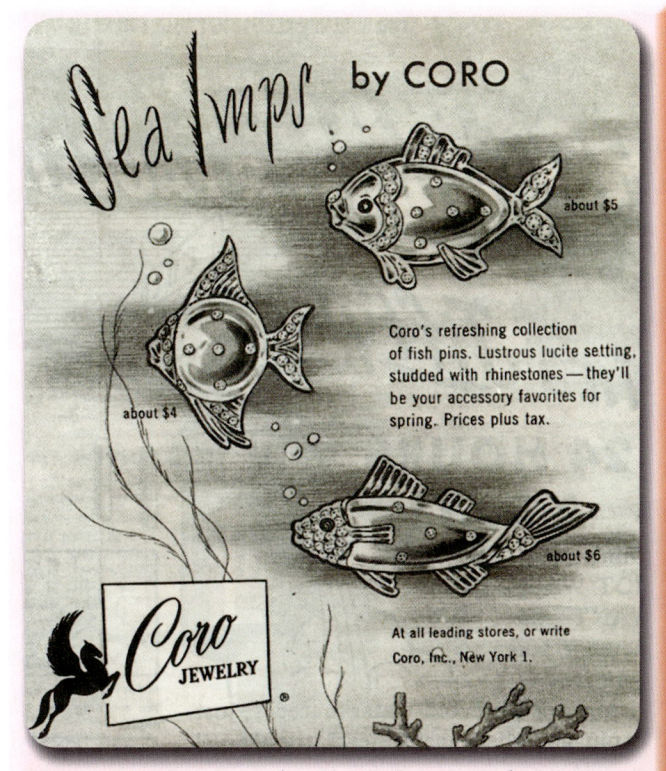

Figure 12. Sea Imps by Coro: Coro jewelry vintage advertisement.

the wealthy, the war affected travel abroad, so vacation fashions were developed for domestic travel. Western wear became very popular. Confined to the western hemisphere, more adventurous travelers set out for Canada and South America. Jewelry designs reflected these new influences. Metals used by the costume jewelry industry came under strict control. Rhinestones were not being imported so their use was limited to existing inventories. American-made pearls were available to make a substantial contribution to costume jewelry designs.

The outputs of costume jewelry manufacturers were governed by quotas that were set by the government. Sterling silver was used to make costume jewelry because by March 1942, costume jewelry manufacturers were told to stop making goods which used a long list of critical metals. For example, rhodium, used to put a tarnish resistant finish on costume jewelry and to alloy platinum, was

ATWOOD & SAWYER	DENICOLA	GOLDETTE	LES BERNARD, MIMI DI NISCEMI	KENNETH J. LANE	AVON	CAROLEE	IAN ST. GIELAR
1956	1957	1958	1962	1963	1971	1972	1989

23

Fashion and Jewelry Timeline

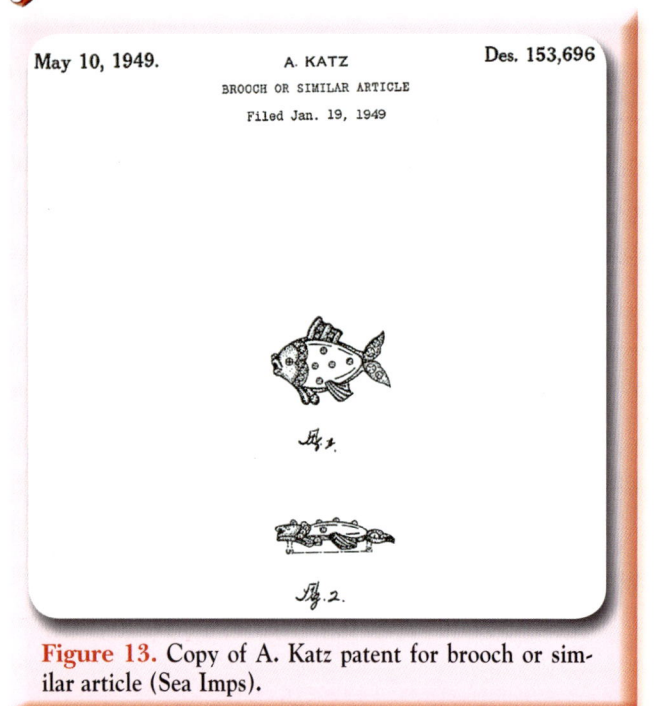

Figure 13. Copy of A. Katz patent for brooch or similar article (Sea Imps).

After 1945, several painters and sculptors began designing jewelry. Among these artists were Alexander Calder, Salvador Dali, and Max Ernst. In 1946, Providence, Rhode Island, was declared the costume jewelry capitol of the United States. Also in the 1940s, the invisible setting, in which stones were fastened from the back to look as if there was no metal mount, was perfected.

The postwar period was dominated by optimism and great prosperity for many Americans. Mass production methods perfected during the war years were used for retail products; a booming economy helped boost markets. Wartime restrictions were relaxed on imported rhinestones leading to their resounding re-emergence in jewelry. Elaborately jeweled bib and collar necklaces dripping with rhinestones become popular and were perfect for accenting the low necklines of evening dresses. Sparkling cocktail jewels resembled shooting stars and fireworks. Lilac, orange, and green faux pearls appeared. Glamour came back in style and frankly fake was "in" again, aided by sparkling aurora borealis rhinestones. In 1953, both Trifari and Coro made crown and scepter brooches in recognition of the coronation of Queen Elizabeth II.

Trifari developed Trifanium, a special alloyed casting metal used to create cast pieces which were then filed, polished, and plated.[9] The process was perfect for satisfying the 1950s craze for ultra-shiny costume gems.

First Lady Mamie Eisenhower commissioned Trifari to design pieces for the 1952 and 1956 Presidential inaugurations. A total of three sets of Mrs. Eisenhower's jewels were made; one can still be seen in the Smithsonian Institute in Washington, D.C. Mrs. Eisenhower was the first wife of a President to wear costume jewelry. Almost three decades later another first lady, Barbara Bush, would create her signature look with the help of several strands of costume jewelry pearls.

Earrings were everywhere and short hair styles were a great complement for gigantic ear bobs. Giant hoops and crystal clusters reminiscent of chandeliers became very popular.

Also during the 1950s the United States became the center of the world's fashion costume jewelry trade. An explosive growth in the production of costume jewelry was due to the increasing use of modern production methods. Experimentation with assembly line set-ups began shortly after World War II. After the cast was made, production moved rapidly. Costume jewelry was more affordable than ever.

Toward the end of the decade, an alternative art jewelry style emerged which included misshapen pearls and irregularly shaped glass stones with mottled surfaces, known as lava stones. These were set into rough or molten-look metal that looked like it had been subjected to an explosion. This alternative style anticipated the unrest of the 1960s.

Boutiques were back in vogue. Space-age plastic rings and strings of ethnic beads became popular. Loose fitting clothes, ethnic jewelry, lots of beads in polished, semi-precious stones or carved wood were worn by both men and women in long strings around the neck. Space age fashions featured sculpted, geometric shapes and employed synthetics including hard plastic and silver lurex.

During the 1960s the boundaries blurred between art and fashion. Designers used pop art and op art as inspiration. The clever use of shapes, including circles, squares, and spirals, gave the illusion of movement. Picasso's cubist faces and Mondrian's geometric designs began appearing on brooches.

The flower was the symbol of natural beauty. Daisy-like flowers in unusual colors such as olive green and bright pink were popular. "Flower power" was about going back to nature. Hippie slogans such as "Peace" and "Love" reflected the desire for alternative ways of living in which individuals could turn away from society's conventions. Typical flower brooches of this era are shown in the photo on the next page.

Indian-inspired costume jewelry became very popular as many famous people made pilgrimages to India to seek spiritual direction, among them the Beatles. Kenneth Jay Lane helped make costume jewelry a sought-after accessory in high society by copying famous and fabulous jewels. The Duchess of Windsor started wearing his pieces during the 1960s.

And then came the 1970s, which has often been called the decade that style forgot. A number of different styles came on the scene. Alternative and anti-fashions

---

[9] "Irving Wolf and Trifari: A View from the Top," by Susan Simon Corwin, *VFCJ*, Vol. 16, No. 3, 2006.

Fashion and Jewelry Timeline

Three large enameled flower pins from the 1960s. Daisies were a popular symbol of the hippie subculture. The olive and fuchsia colors of the other brooches help date the pins as well. $15.00 – 25.00.

abounded, and many people believed the 1970s would be the end of haute couture. Designers began instead to focus on ready-to-wear fashions including fitness apparel.

Anti-fashion showed up in offices as women abandoned traditional ideals of feminine fashion. By selecting clothes and accessories that were not overly feminine, women in the workplace were dressing for success in the business world. They wore conservatively styled suits in gray or navy blue. Fashions were serious and understated. Jewelry was small and tailored if it was worn at all.

Punk fashions also appeared. Jewelry, if it could be called jewelry, was worn everywhere. Pushing safety pins through cheeks, ears, and every available area of clothing challenged conventional notions of good taste. A 1976 Italian *Vogue* featured pages of black clothing worn with aggressive accessories except that the safety pins were made of 14K gold.

By the 1980s, costume jewelry enjoyed a renaissance of gigantic proportions. Designs became glamorous, witty, and more exciting than ever before. Everything was back in style including rhinestones and oversized pearls. The best pearls came from Hong Kong, Japan, and Spain.

Growing interest in collecting and wearing early costume jewelry took hold during the 1980s. Of special interest was the work of Trifari, Boucher, and Haskell.

Atwood and Sawyer, a British firm, supplied much of the jewelry for the *Dallas* and *Dynasty* television shows. The Dynasty collection, an assortment of fabulous fakes, was inspired by Krystle Carrington from *Dynasty*. Butler and Wilson, another British company, made stunning, creative, and oversized costume jewelry pieces.

Glamour was back in style and with it came some of the most fabulous costume jewelry ever made. By the mid-1980s it was a booming $2.3 billion a year industry.

Costume jewelry began to look more and more like the real thing as the craze for glamour escalated. In 1987, the auctions of Diana Vreeland's costume jewelry and the Duchess of Windsor's jewels set off a spate of imitations. Kenneth Jay Lane and Carolee Friedlander, among others, were quick to realize the value of translating the Windsor treasures into affordable costume jewelry. In 1988, Sotheby's sale of Andy Warhol's Bakelite jewelry collection caused a sensation and prices skyrocketed.

Due to its relentless popularity, more designers than ever were making costume jewelry. The ranks included Anne Klein, Givenchy, Emanuel Ungaro, Yves Saint Laurent, Bill Blass, and Oscar de la Renta. Customers could choose flashy brooches, shoe clips, lapel pins, earrings, necklaces, and even hat pins.

The final decade of the century saw the revival of many fashions of past decades as the popularity of costume jewelry continued. Liz Taylor designed jewelry for Avon. Jose Barrera and Kenneth Jay Lane also designed for Avon. Their designs were fabulous, affordable, and highly collectible.

Vintage Fashion and Costume Jewelry began publishing a quarterly magazine as collectors searched for more and more information. The landmark 1992 Jewels of Fantasy exhibit traveled the globe. The exhibit's catalog became an instant hit. It continues to be sought after by collectors of costume jewelry.

In December of 1998 at the Treadway Gallery Auction a Bakelite and wood "Pumpkin Man" pin, 5" tall, sold for an astounding $21,000.00 defying auction house estimates.

Collecting costume jewelry had become an international pastime. Carla Ginelli Brunialti and Roberto Brunialti brought new meaning to the word "research" in their fabulous reviews of the history of American costume jewelry.

By the year 2000, prices for certain costume jewelry pieces were defying all projections. At Doyle's auction on November 1 – 2, 2000, of the Maselli collections, a group of red and yellow Bakelite bracelets, three with heavy carving, sold for a whopping $14,950![10]

An unsigned brass collar attributed to Alexander Calder sold for $31,080, while a lot of 10 Trifari enameled figural pins sold for $3,450. A group of four Trifari jelly belly pins sold for $7,475.

In 2004, at Doyle's twice-yearly couture, textiles, and accessories auction, a mint-condition Chanel sautoir and oblong pendant, circa 1935, in silver-plated metal set with rhinestones and imitation emeralds, sold for $1,500. In 2005, at Juliens Auctions in Los Angeles, a Kenneth Jay Lane tiger bracelet sold for $540.

In 2007, the Providence, Rhode Island, museum of costume jewelry was declared a national museum affirming the place of costume jewelry manufacturing in our nation's history. Today, the number and quality of costume jewelry identification and price guides continues to grow helping to ensure that collectors are more well informed than ever.

---

[10] The Embezzler's Bakelite: The Masellis Sales. From the *Maine Antique Digest: The Americana Chronicles*, edited by Lita Solis – Cohen.

Brooches

Reds

This pretty layered brooch has red stones and measures 3" in diameter. It features seven very large pear-shaped rhinestones; each one measures an inch long. All stones in this magnificent brooch are prong-set. Unsigned. $45.00 – 70.00.

A huge gold-tone symmetrical brooch by Sarah Coventry features an olive green cabochon center, surrounded by four red cabochons and four large red, blue, green, and yellow dappled design cabochons. This piece was named Mosaic and made its debut along with matching earrings in the late 1960s. It measures 3" across and is signed ©SARAHCOV. $25.00 – 40.00.

This unsigned brooch with ruby red rhinestones measures over 3½" long. All of the stones are prong-set. Four gold-tone flowers set with chaton-cut red rhinestones run the length of the brooch. Even the stems are set with tiny red rhinestones. $50.00 – 75.00.

Brooches: Reds

Maltese cross brooch is trimmed with red velvet and enamel and features a central faux turquoise cabochon, red rhinestones, seed pearls, and small turquoise colored cabochons. The pin measures 2" across and is signed ©ART. $60.00 – 80.00.

On the upper left, a large brooch with silver-tone lattice design is set with red rhinestones. A fly is sitting on the upper section. Signed DODDZ. $35.00 – 50.00. The smaller pin is very similar in design and features a small butterfly decorated with pearls. The butterfly sits on the right hand side of the pin. Signed DODDZ. $25.00 – 35.00.

Beautiful enamel Maltese cross with large red center stone is encircled by smaller clear rhinestones. The clear rhinestones are prong-set in a japanned setting. The pin measures 2½" in diameter and is signed ©HAR. HAR enamel jewelry is very well made and still moderately priced relative to other HAR pieces. $50.00 – 75.00.

Brooches: Reds

Another example of HAR jewelry, this striking brooch features a large center speckled stone encircled by smaller, similar stones. The ornate gold-tone setting is made in two pieces. The brooch measures 2½" x 2¾" and is marked ©HAR. $60.00 – 75.00.

This swirl design brooch has lovely pink and red rhinestones in a shiny gold-tone setting. All stones are prong-set in this high quality brooch. Unsigned. $45.00 – 60.00.

Weiss brooch features pink and red rhinestones in the shape of a flower in an antiqued gold-tone setting. The pin is marked WEISS on an oval cartouche. $50.00 – 75.00.

Brooches: Reds

Pink and red rhinestones are featured in this pretty pin in a detailed gold-tone setting. The pin measures 2" in diameter and is signed ©LISNER. $35.00 – 50.00.

Cranberry colored crystals and prong-set aurora borealis rhinestones are featured in this pretty gold-tone brooch. It measures 2" in diameter and is marked MADE IN AUSTRIA. From the standpoint of style and materials, jewelry made in Austria rivals other top quality costume jewelry. The prices of this type of jewelry are steadily rising. $45.00 – 60.00.

Pretty red chaton-cut rhinestones and tiny turquoise colored cabochons are featured in an antiqued silver-tone setting. Measuring almost 2" across, this lovely brooch can also be worn as a pendant. Marked FLORENZA© on raised rectangle. $50.00 – 75.00.

Brooches: Reds

Gorgeous wreath-shaped brooch decorated with pearls in antiqued gold-tone setting measures 2¼" across. Beautiful prong-set purple, red, blue, pink, green, topaz, and aurora borealis rhinestones are accented with pearls and gold-tone curlicues. Marked MADE IN AUSTRIA on an oval cartouche. $45.00 – 60.00.

Weiss brooch features the colors of autumn including gold, red, and orange rhinestones in an antiqued gold-tone setting. The pin measures 2" x 2½" and is signed ©WEISS on an oval cartouche. $50.00 – 75.00.

Open victory wreath design has deep red and aurora borealis rhinestones in a shiny rhodium setting. All of the stones are prong-set except for the smaller aurora borealis stones extending from the center stone. It measures 2¼" at its widest point. Unsigned. $40.00 – 60.00.

Brooches: Reds

Star-shaped brooch features pink and red prong-set rhinestones in a gold-tone setting. Unsigned. $30.00 – 45.00.

This classic circle pin features red rhinestones in a silver setting. Floating wires overlap from the back of the pin to front. Each ends in a small heart. Marked Sterling. $45.00 – 60.00.

Delizza and Elster (Juliana) musical brooch measures almost 3" long. All of the ruby red rhinestones are prong-set in bright gold-tone and trimmed with aurora borealis rhinestones. Unsigned. $45.00 – 60.00.

Brooches: Reds

Victorian revival cross is trimmed with pearls and ruby red rhinestones in an ornate gold-tone setting. The cross measures 2½" long and 1¾" wide. It has a bail so it can also be worn on a chain. Unsigned. $35.00 – 50.00.

Quirky question mark brooch measures 2½" long and features red and aurora borealis rhinestones in various sizes. It is stamped MADE IN AUSTRIA on the back. It is also marked STAR on an oval cartouche. $45.00 – 60.00. When I asked Pat Seal about these two marks, she sent me a picture of a brooch from her collection that was marked both KRAMER and MADE IN AUSTRIA, noting that some Kramer jewelry was made in Austria. She was unaware that selected Star jewelry pieces were made in Austria. Evidently it was and we both learned something.

Pink and lavender rhinestones are in a gold-tone setting featuring a pretty leaf design. The brooch measures 2" in diameter and is unsigned. $25.00 – 35.00.

Brooches: Blues

This lovely circle pin has a gold ribbon design. The pin measures 2" in diameter and has two sizes of chaton-cut aurora borealis rhinestones. Unsigned. $25.00 – 35.00.

This large brooch measures 2" x 2½" and features raspberry and peach beads individually strung, prong-set rhinestones, and iridescent leaves. The brooch is signed in two places: STANLEY HAGLER N.Y.C. on an oval cartouche, on another cartouche it is signed IAN St. GIELAR. $200.00 – 250.00. Ian St. Gielar made jewelry that has been described as "wearable works of art." He began working with Stanley Hagler in 1989 and left the company around 1994. He died unexpectedly in March 2007 from complications following a car accident.

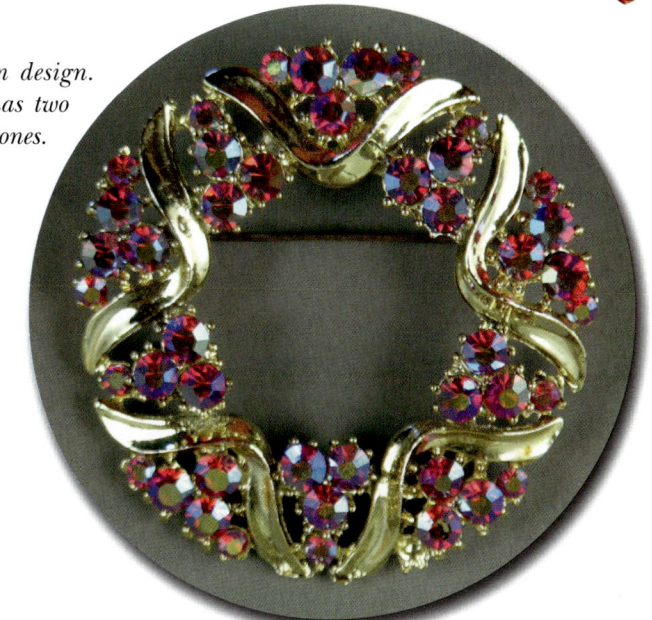

Blues

There simply aren't enough adjectives to describe this Joseff of Hollywood brooch. Joseff mostly produced jewelry that he rented to the studios for films. He used a matte gold finish because it didn't reflect in powerful studio lights. This brooch has his characteristic finish. The rhinestones are a beautiful clear blue, unfoiled, with open backs. This magnificent piece measures 3" x 2¼". Joseff jewelry proved to be so popular that he also marketed a line of costume jewelry for sale in boutiques. This beauty can be worn as a brooch as shown in the photograph or it can be worn as a pendant. The design on the bottom of the brooch doubles as a bail for a completely different look. Signed JOSEFF HOLLYWOOD on an oval cartouche. $250.00 – 300.00.

Brooches: Blues

This lovely brooch measures a whopping 3¾" across. The classic design makes it appear at first to be much older than it is. Amazingly this heavy pin does not have a bail; I could imagine it being worn as a pendant because of its weight. It features royal blue and clear rhinestones in a silver-tone setting. The center stone is a full 1" long! It is signed ©GRAZIANO on an oval cartouche. $50.00 – 75.00. Robert Graziano has been making jewelry since the early 1970s. His designs include necklaces, bracelets, brooches, earrings, and rings. His styles incorporate top quality materials including Swarovski rhinestones.

This lovely pin is surprisingly unsigned. However, it is very similar to a signed Hattie Carnegie piece that I have seen. It features a large center glass stone measuring 2" and is surrounded by molded glass stones that look like leaves and smaller blue rhinestones that are all prong-set. The large blue center stone is attached with floating wires. $75.00 – 100.00.

Brooch with pale blue rhinestones in a rainbow design. The larger blue marquis-shaped rhinestones are unfoiled in an open back silver-tone setting; the largest rhinestones are ¾" long. The small square rhinestones are aurora borealis and all are prong-set. $45.00 – 60.00.

Brooches: Blues

This brooch with green, amber, and blue stones in a silver-tone setting. The rhinestones are all prong-set and the marquis-shaped stones around the edge have open backs showing unfoiled rhinestones. The pin measures 2½" across, and some of the stones are molded to look like leaves. It was probably made by DeLizza and Elster (Juliana). Typical D&E characteristics include open backed, unfoiled rhinestones, navette shaped stones, rhodium plated metal, and distinctive center stones. D&E jewelry was marked with a hang tag which was removed before wearing. Occasionally lucky collectors will find a piece or set with original hang tags. Unsigned. $45.00 – 65.00.

Huge brooch with varying shades of blue rhinestones, all shapes and sizes, and all prong-set. The brooch, set in creamy rhodium, measures a whopping 3" across! Unsigned. $50.00 – 75.00.

This pretty crown brooch measures over 2" across. The large center navy blue cabochon is encircled with clear, prong-set rhinestones. The tip of the crown is also decorated with clear rhinestones; the pin features faux turquoise navettes and smaller blue cabochons. Top to bottom the crown measures 2¼". Unsigned. $35.00 – 60.00.

35

Brooches: Blues

Beautiful brooch with large blue cabochon stone in the center. This is a very substantial and dimensional brooch measuring over 2" across. Note the three lovely flowers; their center cabochons are encircled with clear prong-set rhinestones. The small blue stones are glued in and match the center stones in the flowers. Unsigned. $40.00 – 65.00.

Leaf and floral design brooch has blue aurora borealis flowers with clear centers in a gold-tone setting. The brooch measures 2½" long x 1½" across. It is signed with the Pegasus symbol and Coro ©. $20.00 – 40.00.

This unsigned beauty measures almost 5" long. The dimensional gold-tone leaf design is made in two pieces and is accented with tiny clear and blue rhinestones. This pin belongs to my mother and dates to the late 1950s. $35.00 – 60.00.

Brooches: Blues

Aurora borealis rhinestones are set in swirling silver-tone. The pin measures 3" in length and is signed ©Coro on a raised rectangle. $20.00 – 45.00.

Lovely unsigned pin features interesting details in the gold-tone setting, including variegated leaves. The pin measures 2½" across. $35.00 – 60.00.

Shimmering oval turquoise colored rhinestones are in a substantial gold-tone setting in the shape of a star. This beautiful brooch is stamped TRIFARI©. The brooch is made in two pieces which are attached with rivets. $50.00 – 75.00.

Brooches: Blues

Pinwheel design rhinestone brooch is signed WIESNER in capital letters on an oval cartouche. Blue marquis rhinestones are framed by a circle of clear rhinestones in a silver-tone setting. Wiesner jewelry is very well constructed and is difficult to find; the pieces I have seen feature high quality rhinestones in classic designs. $50.00 – 75.00.

Pretty CORO fur clip measures 1½" tall, and has channel set turquoise and clear rhinestones. Note the tiny flowers towards the bottom of the clip. The signature can be found on the back on a raised rectangle. It includes the Pegasus symbol and Coro in script. $35.00 – 50.00.

Matte gold-tone snowflake with tiny, pale blue rhinestones measures 2" across and is signed ©DODDZ. $35.00 – 50.00.

Brooches: Blues

Chatelaines were an important part of the Victorian household and were both ornamental and prestigious. They were worn by the mistress of the house and were used to carry important household items such as keys, a watch, scissors, a knife, coin purse, etc. Inspired by Victorian necessity, this much later version features center blue chaton-cut rhinestones in a heavy gold-tone setting. The piece measures 9" from end to end. Unsigned. $20.00 – 30.00.

Weiss brooch with clear blue rhinestones features two large teardrop shaped rhinestones at the bottom of the victory wreath design. The pin is signed WEISS on an oval cartouche with no copyright symbol dating it to before 1955. $50.00 – 75.00.

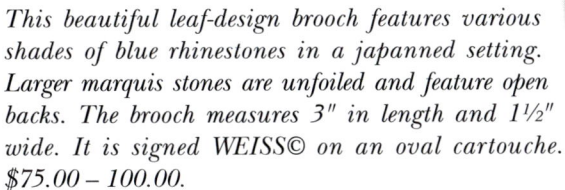

This beautiful leaf-design brooch features various shades of blue rhinestones in a japanned setting. Larger marquis stones are unfoiled and feature open backs. The brooch measures 3" in length and 1½" wide. It is signed WEISS© on an oval cartouche. $75.00 – 100.00.

39

Brooches: Blues

Silver-tone leaf design brooch has an unusual shade of blue rhinestones. All of the stones are the same clear royal blue color. Unsigned. $20.00 – 35.00.

Carnival glass telephone scatter pins have light green rhinestones in the dial and a large yellow center rhinestone. A sweet set. Unsigned. $20.00 – 35.00.

Fabulous paisley design swirl brooch measures 1¾" long. It features two outer rows of pale blue stones, a third row of darker blue stones, followed by a row of green and a row of pale yellow stones for a total of 180 prong-set stones! The brooch is signed in an oval cartouche LES BERNARD, INC. $75.00 – 100.00.

Brooches: Blues

Unsigned, silver-tone umbrella with colored rhinestones. The silver-tone glistens as though it is wet. This brooch was designed and made for the New Jersey Order of the Eastern Star (1985). It was named Showers of Blessings. $15.00 – 25.00.

Pale and royal blue prong-set rhinestones are featured in this brooch that reminds me of a sideways comma. Unsigned. $35.00 – 60.00.

Graceful blue rhinestone brooch in a shiny rhodium setting; the center of the brooch is accented by a large, dark blue rhinestone. Unsigned. $35.00 – 60.00.

41

Brooches: Blues

Clear and colored rhinestones adorn this brooch. The small, clear rhinestones are pavé set on the leaves and stem alternating with red, green, purple, and cognac-colored marquis-shaped stones in a rhodium setting. Unsigned. $35.00 – 60.00.

Aurora borealis round and baguette rhinestones adorn the surface of this graceful brooch featuring a hand holding a cocktail glass. The setting is shiny rhodium, still bright after many years. Hand brooches are always popular with collectors. Since this is a family piece, I can date it with confidence to the late 1950s. The signature is stamped on the back of the brooch ©PELL. $100.00 – 125.00.

Blue and lavender aurora borealis rhinestones are featured in a rhodium setting in the shape of a victory wreath. The brooch measures almost 2½" across. Unsigned. $25.00 – 50.00.

Brooches: Blues

Mid-1950s circle pin is similar to design patent #155681 issued October 25, 1949, to Marcel Boucher (see Figure 14). This is one of many variations on the circle pin design produced by Boucher. It features sapphire color baguettes and small clear rhinestones which give this petite brooch the look of fine jewelry. Measuring just 1½" wide, it is signed ©BOUCHER. Note the buckle design at the top of the pin. $50.00 – 75.00.

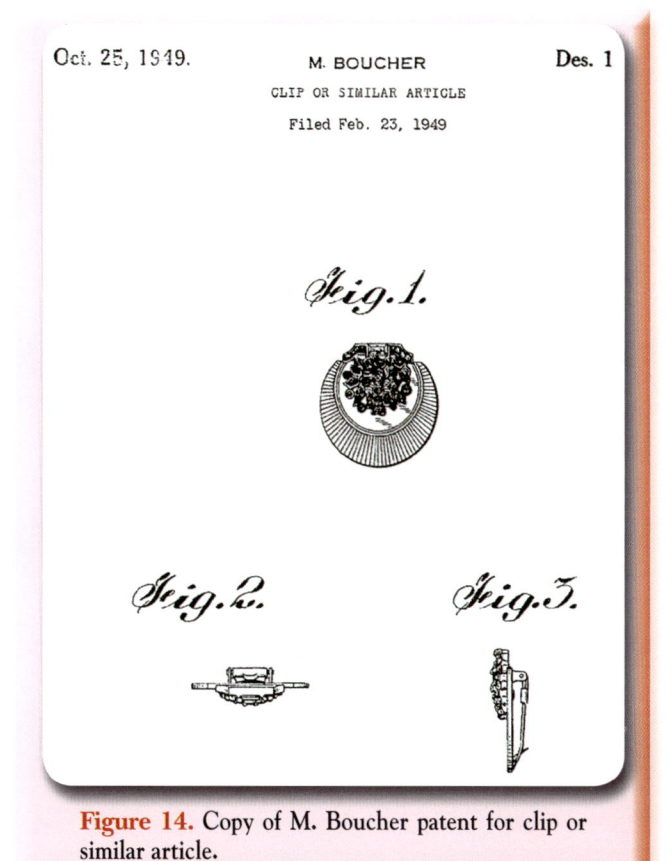

Figure 14. Copy of M. Boucher patent for clip or similar article.

Domed brooch with a large emerald cut black rhinestone and smaller marquis combine with varying sizes of aurora borealis rhinestones to create a dramatic effect. The brooch measures 2½" across and sits ¾" high. Most likely this is a DeLizza & Elster piece. $75.00 – 100.00.

43

Brooches: Blues

Prong-set faux turquoise and pale blue stones are featured in this unusual brooch; some of stones are molded glass. The brooch measures 2¼" in diameter. Unsigned. $50.00 – 75.00.

Round brooch in gold-tone setting has dramatic cat's eye stones. Measuring 1¾" across, this pretty brooch is accented with pale blue and green chaton-cut rhinestones. The focal point is a large and lovely stone that reminds me of a paperweight. Unsigned. $35.00 – 60.00.

Greens

Brooch featuring gold-tone leaves and huge center unfoiled rhinestone with open back. Marquis-shaped rhinestones in alternating light and dark shades of green are dotted with aurora borealis stones to set off this beautiful wreath-shaped brooch which resembles a DeLizza and Elster design. All of the stones are prong-set; the brooch measures almost 2" across. In mid-2007, DeLizza and Elster jewelry is sought after by collectors of vintage costume jewelry. The more unusual stones, the better! Actually, D&E jewelry was mostly made for other companies except for about a two year period (1967 – 1968) when D&E marketed a line of costume jewelry under their name. See ad from the 1960 Jeweler's Buyers Guide in Figure 15. Unsigned. $75.00 – 100.00.

Brooches: Greens

Figure 15. DeLizza and Elster advertisement from the 1960 *Jewelers' Buyers Guide*.

DeLizza and Elster Juliana-style brooch with loads of detail including two beautifully carved stones accented with rhinestones. The brooch also has prong-set aurora borealis, emerald green, orange, golden topaz, and olive green rhinestones. It measures 2¼" at the widest point. A real stunner. $75.00 – 100.00.

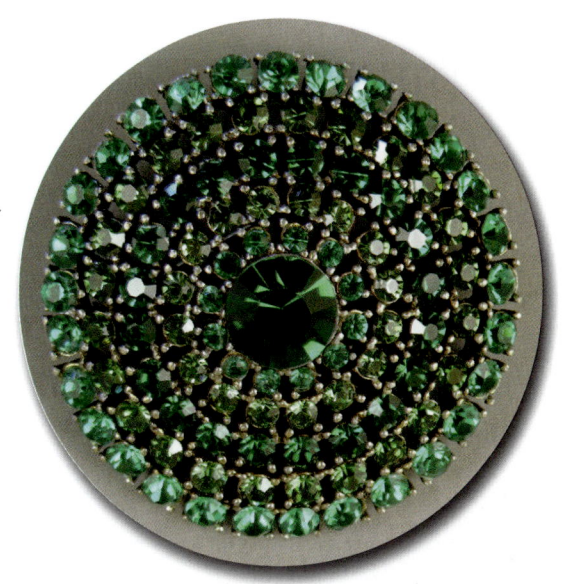

Beautiful Weiss pin is set with emerald green rhinestones. The center foiled rhinestone has an open back. The brooch measures 1¾" in diameter and reminds me of the Rondo brooch featured in the ad in Figure 16. Signed ©WEISS. $75.00 – 100.00.

45

Brooches: Greens

Figure 16. Weiss vintage advertisement from 1954 Vogue magazine.

Long and languid, this gorgeous reticulated brooch measures almost 4" in length. It features beautiful blue and green navette shaped rhinestones, all prong-set. Unsigned. $75.00 – 100.00.

Art Deco style pin has lovely emerald green baquettes and clear pavé rhinestones in a rhodium setting. The pin has the look of fine jewelry and is signed WIESNER on an oval cartouche. $50.00 – 75.00.

Brooches: Greens

This brooch has green and blue marquis-shaped rhinestones around a large blue center stone in gold-tone setting. Some of the rhinestones have open backs; the pin measures almost 2" across. Unsigned. $40.00 – 65.00.

Kramer brooch featuring luscious blue and green rhinestones. The brooch measures 2½" long x 2" wide, and is marked KRAMER on an oval cartouche. $75.00 – 100.00.

Unsigned brooch with a brilliant cut, center unfoiled rhinestone which is prong-set. The center green stone measures a full 1" in diameter. The gold-tone setting resembles a wreath with leaves; the brooch measures 2" across. $60.00 – 85.00.

47

Brooches: Greens

This heavy and dimensional brooch has glued-in green rhinestones featuring open backs in a substantial gold-tone setting. The brooch measures ¾" high and 2½" across. $35.00 – 60.00.

An unusual rectangular-shaped brooch with peridot, emerald, and aurora borealis, prong-set rhinestones is accented with enameled leaves. Some of the rhinestones in this well-constructed pin are in raised filigree settings. The pin is marked MADE AUSTRIA (not a typo!) on the pin mechanism. $50.00 – 75.00.

A popular circle-pin design with an unusual presentation. Each of the aurora borealis rhinestones are mounted in cone-shaped individual settings for a very geometric effect. The pin is marked WEISS in an oval cartouche and measures 2" across. $50.00 – 75.00.

Brooches: Greens

Gold-tone rope design in a free-form setting features smooth, pear-shaped green stones. Measuring 2¼" across, the pin is marked DALSHEIM© on an oval cartouche. $40.00 – 65.00.

Lovely dangling style brooch has emerald green foiled marquis-shaped rhinestones in a shiny gold-tone setting accented with clear rhinestones. Note the line of clear rhinestones across the top of the bar. The pin measures 2½" across (top bar) and 2½" from top to bottom. It is signed Coro Craft (each word on a separate line) in a raised rectangle. $60.00 – 85.00.

This petite pin has a large center marble-look stone, accented with tiny green rhinestones in an antiqued gold-tone setting. Signed FLORENZA©. $25.00 – 40.00.

49

Brooches: Greens

An ornate looped gold-tone setting is featured in this lovely brooch. The center is loaded with blue/green rhinestones. Signed KARU ARKÉ Inc. $35.00 – 60.00.

This very dimensional pin measures 1" deep x 2" wide. The outer ring of emerald green rhinestones are marquis shaped and unfoiled with open backs. The next ring is lovely aurora borealis accented with square pale green colored stones. Unsigned. $35.00 – 60.00.

This leaf pin has pale blue and green rhinestones set in gold-tone setting. Unsigned. $25.00 – 40.00.

50

BROOCHES: GREENS

A piece of wearable art, this stunning hand-beaded brooch is signed in two places including STANLEY HAGLER NYC on one oval cartouche and on another IAN St. GEILAR. $175.00 – 250.00.

This unsigned pin has poured glass flower petals and stamped metal leaves. Provenance dates this pin to 1941 – 1942. It measures 2½" high and the center of the flower is decorated with a clear stone. $35.00 – 50.00.

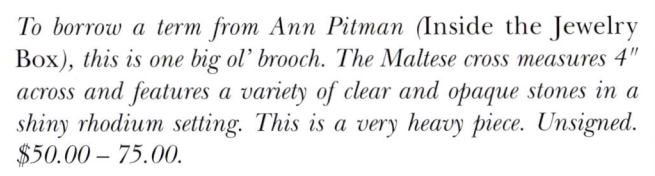

To borrow a term from Ann Pitman (Inside the Jewelry Box), this is one big ol' brooch. The Maltese cross measures 4" across and features a variety of clear and opaque stones in a shiny rhodium setting. This is a very heavy piece. Unsigned. $50.00 – 75.00.

51

Brooches: Black Diamonds and Patriotic Jewelry

"Black Diamonds" and Patriotic Jewelry

[11] The phrase black diamonds refers to faux smoky quartz stones; the term was originally used in Weiss jewelry ads.

Navette and round rhinestones are featured in a gold-tone setting. This pin is signed AUSTRIA on an oval cartouche and measures 1¾" across. It features black and gray rhinestones, all prong-set. $50.00 – 75.00.

This well made brooch has an antiqued silver-tone setting and features shimmering gray rhinestones. Signed HOLLYCRAFT COPR 1954. $50.00 – 75.00.

This beautiful brooch features a large center chaton-cut black diamond and smaller aurora borealis and gray navettes. Most of the stones in this pretty piece are prong-set. It is amazingly lightweight for its size; it measures 2" across. The style of this brooch is consistent with the style of Beau Jewels. It is made with high quality materials. Another design characteristic of Beau Jewels is a filigree centerpiece with lightweight branches of metal riveted together. Some Beau Jewels pieces incorporate molded stones into their designs. Brooches are not signed; earrings are usually signed. This piece is unsigned. $50.00 – 75.00.

Brooches: Black Diamonds and Patriotic Jewelry

This stacked brooch measures 1" deep x 2" across. It features 12 heart-shaped clear stones, black plastic inserts, and aurora borealis rhinestones in the center. Unsigned. $50.00 – 75.00.

Smooth and faceted marquis-shaped frosted stones are featured in this lovely silver-tone brooch. The flower centers are aurora borealis stones which are also placed throughout the brooch. It measures 2½" at its widest. Unsigned. $40.00 – 60.00.

S-shaped brooch has round and baguette-shaped black diamonds, accented with aurora borealis rhinestones in a rhodium setting. Unsigned. $40.00 – 60.00.

53

Brooches: Black Diamonds and Patriotic Jewelry

This leaf design brooch features prong-set black diamonds and aurora borealis rhinestones. The outer rhinestones along the border have open backs. Unsigned. $40.00 – 60.00.

Large brooch resembles a spray of flowers and leaves; it is accented with aurora borealis rhinestones. The pin also features prong-set marquis, navette, and chaton-cut clear and gray rhinestones. Large and lightweight, it measures 3½" across. The brooch has many characteristics of Beau Jewels jewelry. Unsigned. $60.00 – 85.00.

Back of brooch reveals characteristic Beau Jewels construction.

Brooches: Black Diamonds and Patriotic Jewelry

Beautiful stacked brooch has large aurora borealis and gray chaton cut rhinstones set in shiny rhodium. It measures ¾" deep and 2½" in diameter. Unsigned. $50.00 – 75.00.

This fabulous, huge brooch measures 3¼" across. It features large chaton-cut aurora borealis rhinestones and smaller chaton and baguette style gray rhinestones. Every stone is prong-set. This is a heavy brooch in a rhodium setting; it is one of my absolute favorites. Unsigned. $100.00 – 125.00.

Left: Rhinestone-studded airplane with blue and red accents. This World War II vintage plane is stamped with the TRIFARI crown signature. Wing span is 2" across. $100.00 – 125.00. Right: Richly detailed petite silver eagle is stamped AMCO Sterling. AMCO jewelry is known for elegant and classic designs. $45.00 – 60.00.

Brooches: Black Diamonds and Patriotic Jewelry

Left: Detailed brooch features two sailors with pearl faces and pavé set clear rhinestones. This pin measures 2" tall. Unsigned. $75.00 – 100.00. In the Brunialtis' book entitled A Tribute to America, *a similar pin is featured and is marked MB (for Marcel Boucher). According to the Brunialtis there was a very similar brooch shown in* LIFE *magazine (February 1940) and in* Glamour *magazine (March 1941) but neither example was signed. Right: Details abound in this uniformed flagman wearing red, white, and blue; he shows a bit of wear. The pin measures 2" tall and is unsigned. $50.00 – 75.00.*

Flowers

Upper left: Pavé set clear rhinestones decorate this flower brooch. Other beautiful details abound in this stunning pin. Note the leaves are tipped with clear rhinestones; a ribbon tying the bouquet together is also trimmed with clear stones. The brooch measures 3½" long. Unsigned. $60.00 – 85.00. Upper right: Beautiful, heavy enamel flower pin signed Coro in script with no copyright symbol. The flower stems are dotted with tiny blue and clear rhinestones in a substantial gold-tone setting. The brooch is made in three pieces and riveted together; it measures 2½" long. $75.00 – 100.00. Bottom: Golden topaz petals with white enameled centers are accented by another golden topaz. Lovely green enameled leaves are featured in a beautiful setting with lots of detail. The brooch measures almost 4" tall. Unsigned. $60.00 – 85.00.

Upper left: Well-made faux smoky quartz and topaz flower brooch with green navettes; petals have open backs; note the detail of tiny golden topaz stones below the leaves. Unsigned. $45.00 – 60.00. Middle: Huge 4" flower with prong-set stones. All stones are the same pale green color set in pretty gold-tone. Unsigned. $45.00 – 60.00. Top right: Milk glass flower has a center of golden topaz. All stones are prong-set; note the tiny green stone on the stem. Unsigned. $45.00 – 60.00. Bottom left: Stunning floral pin features green, open back, heart-shaped rhinestones surrounded by aurora borealis stones. All are prong-set. Unsigned. $45.00 – 60.00. Bottom right: Cognac-colored stones make up the flower in this pretty pin. The same color baguettes are channel set in the stem. Unsigned. $30.00 – 45.00.

Brooches: Flowers

Left: Beautiful flower pin is made with lavender prong-set rhinestones and a middle chaton-cut fuchsia stone with two shades of green leaves. This pin was featured in a 1961 ad which describes several floral brooches as "long-stemmed beauties." Signed WEISS. $60.00 – 75.00. Right: Hard to believe this beauty is not signed. Open back golden topaz colored stones form the petals of the fancy, prong-set flowers. They are accented by enameled petals which include pearl and rhinestone accents. Note the green enamel and rhinestone on the stem. The brooch measures 2" tall x 2½" wide. Unsigned. $50.00 – 75.00.

Upper left: This is one of those pins that makes one realize B.S.K. is undervalued in today's market. It is a substantial and pretty sunflower design with alternating shiny and matte finish gold-tone petals that add texture and interest. Small orange plastic cabochons are set into the flower's center. The brooch is made in two parts and riveted together; it measures 2¼" in diameter. Signed © B.S.K. on raised rectangle. $35.00 – 50.00. Upper right: The large green enamel daisy features a smaller flower on stem. The flower's center is a bright green plastic cabochon. The pin measures just over 3" and is signed WEISS© on an oval cartouche. $50.00 – 75.00. Lower left: Pretty blue enamel daisy with lighter blue cabochon center signed ©WEISS in an oval cartouche. This pin measures 2¾" long. $50.00 – 75.00. Lower right: Turquoise blue marquis with green enamel trim and orange metal center brooch is made in two parts and measures 2" at widest. It is stamped CAPRI in script but I cannot determine if there is a © symbol. $35.00 – 50.00.

Left to right: Pink and green enameled flower brooch has tiny pearls dotting the inside of the flower. The pin is made in two parts and signed on an oval cartouche KRAMER of NEW YORK. $35.00 – 50.00. Closed yellow enameled rose is signed ©SANDOR which is stamped into the metal of the pin mechanism. $25.00 – 35.00. Pale and shimmering, this flower pin features yellow enamel and delicate turquoise cabochons, clear rhinestones, and subtle green enameled leaves. It is marked Coro with © on a raised rectangle. $50.00 – 75.00. Red enamel rose is decorated with tiny clear rhinestones bordering the front leaf. It is signed Capri on an oval cartouche with no copyright symbol dating it to between 1952 and 1955.[12] $35.00 – 60.00.

[12] Carroll, Julia C., *Collecting Costume Jewelry 202: The Basics of Dating Jewelry 1935 – 1980*. Collectors Books, Paducah, KY, 2007.

Brooches: Flowers

Upper middle: A spray of pearls is featured in this matte gold-tone setting with lots of detail. This extremely well made brooch is consistent with the quality collectors associate with HAR jewelry. It measures 2½" x 2½". Signed ©HAR. $60.00 – 75.00. Lower left: Sunflower design brooch has both gold-tone and silver accents and bumble bee detail. The pin measures 1¾" in diameter and is signed LC (for Liz Claiborne). $30.00 – 45.00. Bottom right: Shimmering matte gold-tone setting features clear rhinestone accents. The pin measures 2" in diameter and is signed ©HAR. $45.00 – 60.00.

Upper left: This detailed basket is filled with flowers accented with colored stones and a single pearl. It is marked STERLING on a raised rectangle and measures 2" x 2". Flowerpot brooches are always popular with collectors. $75.00 – 100.00. Beautiful pot of flowers featuring enameled leaves and flowers as well as rhinestone flowers with pearl accents. The brooch measures about 2½" top to bottom. Unsigned. $75.00 – 100.00.

Upper left: Detail abounds in this graceful gold-tone and rhinestone flower. All of the golden topaz colored stones are prong-set. It measures 2" x 3" tall. Signed WEISS on an oval cartouche. $50.00 – 75.00. Upper right: Flowing floral brooch with clear cascading rhinestones has a shiny gold-tone setting. This lovely pin measures 2" tall x 1½" wide. Surprisingly unsigned. $35.00 – 60.00. Lower left: Boucher gold-tone carnation with simple pearl center, a classic and elegant design. The pin measures 3" tall and is signed CARNATION with an inventory number. $50.00 – 75.00. Center: It is hard to believe this beauty is not signed. Measuring almost 3" tall x 2" wide, this lovely layered red flower brooch features petals decorated with prong-set ruby red rhinestones and a clear rhinestone center. The pin is trimmed along its edges with clear and red rhinestones. Unsigned. $50.00 – 75.00. Lower right: Shiny gold-tone is the setting for this beautiful brooch featuring a large pearl center and pavé set rhinestones. Signed Hobé with a copyright symbol over the "o." $50.00 – 75.00.

Brooches: Birds

Left to right: Beautiful red rose is in a gold-tone setting. The pin measures 2½" tall and is marked CERRITO©. $20.00 – 35.00. Elaborate and detailed gold-tone rose pin measures 2" in diameter. Including the stem, the pin measures 2½" long. It is marked ©Coro on a raised rectangle. $25.00 – 40.00. Gold-tone wishbone brooch is made in two pieces (the center rose is one piece). The wishbone is a symbol of good luck; this one is marked Coro in script with no copyright symbol. $25.00 – 40.00. Petite gold and faux ivory bouquet measures just 2" x 1½" wide. The flowers are very detailed in this pretty pin. Signed 1/20 K.G (F may be there but is illegible). The pin also has a CA with an arrow through it, the signature of Carl-Art. $30.00 – 45.00.

Top left: Pretty diamante floral brooch with cross is a brooch from the New Jersey Chapter of the Order of the Eastern Star, year unknown. Unsigned. $20.00 – 30.00. Top right: Heart and rose diamante brooch was the New Jersey's Chapter of the Order of the Eastern Star pin for the year 1967 – 1968. Unsigned. $20.00 – 30.00. Middle: Enameled flower fur clip has pavé rhinestone center and tiny rhinestones accenting the flower petals. The clip measures 3" across and is unsigned. $50.00 – 75.00. Lower left: Silver-tone basket of flowers has clear rhinestone accents. This pretty pin is another example from the New Jersey Order of the Eastern Star. This was the pin of the year for 1970 – 1971. $20.00 – 30.00. Lower right: Diamante flower brooch, unsigned. $25.00 – 40.00.

Birds

Large brooch features a gold-tone setting with plastic inserts and purple rhinestone trim. The blue plastic is molded to look like feathers; the blue enamel on the toucan's tail is dotted with clear rhinestones as is the bird's perch. The beak is a pretty ivory colored plastic. This brooch was one of the pieces given to me by my aunt. The style and quality are consistent with figural jewelry made by Hattie Carnegie. However, this piece is not signed. $100.00 – 125.00.

Brooches: Birds

Majestic heron has clear rhinestones, cream colored enamel, and a tiny green rhinestone eye. Plastic inserts are featured on the body, head, and neck. Clear rhinestones accent the perch. Although this piece is unsigned, it is very similar to a Hattie Carnegie design. $100.00 – 125.00.

Beautiful green and blue enamel with clear rhinestone trim accent this lovely 3½" highly stylized cockatoo in a pot-metal setting. It is unsigned except for the number 10622 shown on a raised rectangle. $50.00 – 75.00.

Gold-tone bird has pearl accents and pretty details in the face and wings. The pin measures 2½" from beak to tail end and is signed ©B.S.K. on a raised rectangle. $25.00 – 40.00.

Brooches: Birds

Unsigned owl with yellow and blue enamel accents measures 2½" tall. This is a heavy and well made brooch with lots of detail including clear rhinestones that encircle the green stone eyes. The shiny gold-tone setting is made in two parts; the eye piece is riveted onto the central base. $25.00 – 40.00.

Glorious crane brooch features a large, beautiful blue center stone and rows of clear rhinestones adorning the feathers. The crane is grooming itself, creating a very dimensional brooch. This is one of those pieces of costume jewelry that you turn over a hundred times looking for a mark or signature. I know because I have done it. Alas, this one is unsigned. $75.00 – 100.00.

This large brooch is signed ©Monet on a raised rectangle and features clear channel set baguettes and a rhinestone body in a pretty gold-tone setting. It measures 4" tall. $35.00 – 60.00.

61

Brooches: Birds

Pot-metal bird with top hat, cane, and green cabochon belly matches a 1941 Coro patent featuring Mr. and Mrs. Bird. Patent #125976 was issued to Gene Verrecchio (Verri) on 3/18/41 (Figure 17). Unsigned. $35.00 – 60.00.

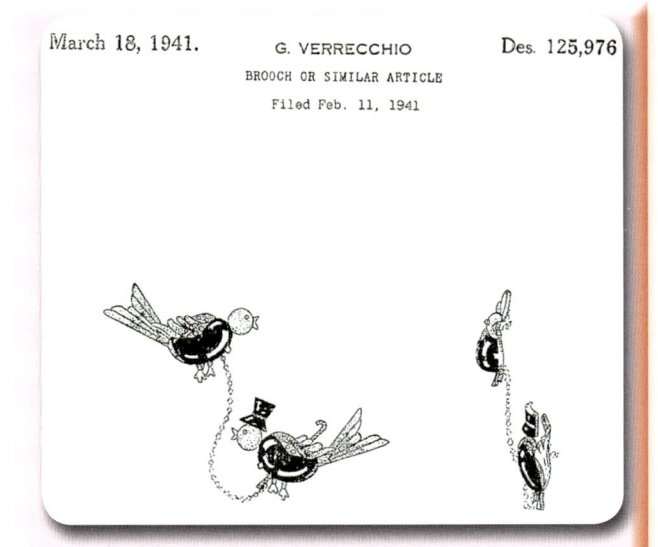

Figure 17. Copy of G. Verrecchio patent for brooch or similar article (Mr. Bird).

White enamel with gold-tone accents are featured on this swallow pin. Coro made several variations of its swallow pin including examples without enamel and with rhinestones. This one measures 2½" in length and is signed with the Pegasus symbol and Coro in script. $35.00 – 60.00.

Brooches: Birds

A pretty blue bird sits near its nest of three pearls in this sweet pin signed GERRY'S©. $20.00 – 35.00.

It is the march of two petite penguins in this 1½" high pin. One penguin sports pavé rhinestones while the other is cream-colored enamel with clear rhinestone trim. The pin is signed CRAFT© on an oval cartouche. $35.00 – 50.00.

This owl charm or pendant with large faux turquoise cabochon belly and pearl eyes is signed Rosenfeld by FLORENZA©. The piece measures 2" from top to bottom. $30.00 – 45.00.

Rosenfeld was a handbag designer and manufacturer located in New York City and a regular Florenza customer from 1960 to 1981. Rosenfeld and Lorraine Marsel (another regular) were the only customers whose names were put on jewelry along with Florenza's. According to Mary Ann Docktor-Smith, an expert in Florenza jewelry, these items were part of Florenza's general merchadise line.

Brooches: Birds

This gold-tone owl is standing tall with large center faux turquoise stone and blue rhinestone eyes. This pretty pin is marked HATTIE CARNEGIE on an oval cartouche. $50.00 – 75.00.

Sarah Coventry gold-tone pin named "Hooter" features greenish yellow aurora borealis stones for eyes and measures 1½" tall. $30.00 – 50.00.

This pin is featured in a 1970 Sara Coventry ad which states "Sarah fashions magic from a walk in the wild." The ad further notes that Sarah Coventry fine fashion jewelry is shown only at "our home jewelry shows."

Under (and around) the Sea

This magnificent turtle brooch features prong-set rhinestones from one end to the other, including a large center foiled rhinestone with open back. It measures almost 3" from head to tail and 2" across including the turtle's feet. The eyes are set on floating wires which originate on the bottom of the brooch. The center rhinestone is 1" long, ¾" wide, and ¼" deep! Unsigned, this is a Juliana piece by DeLizza and Elster. $125.00 – 150.00.

Brooches: Under (and around) the Sea

Upper left: Unsigned beauty features small faux turquoise cabochons, and sapphire and ruby rhinestones in the shape of flowers, with tiny seed pearl centers in a gold-tone setting. The turtle's head and feet are covered in seed pearls. $25.00 – 40.00. Upper right: Tiny gold-tone turtle with pavé set clear rhinestones is accented with tiny red, green, and blue cabochons and one large green cabochon. The turtle measures 1½" x 1¼". $20.00 – 35.00. Lower left: Gold-tone filigree setting has a large center citrine-colored stone encircled with faux jade prong-set cabochons and red rhinestone eyes in a stunning combination of color and textures. This pin measures 2½" x 1¼" and is signed Judith Green in script on an oval cartouche. Judith Green jewelry was sold in better department stores, including Bloomingdale's, in the 1960s. $40.00 – 60.00.[13] Lower right: Tiny gold-tone turtle covered with clear rhinestones and featuring small red rhinestone eyes. It is signed ROMAN on a raised rectangle. $25.00 – 40.00.

[13] Bloomingdale's advertisement, *New York Times*, August 16, 1964.

A grand and heavy gold-tone clam shell has a single pearl accent. The large brooch measures 2¾" x 2¾" and also features a bail so it can be worn as a pendant. It is signed ©Hobé on an oval cartouche. $50.00 – 75.00. Different companies often produced their own interpretations of popular motifs including butterflies, bugs, fish, and Egyptian revival jewelry among many other themes. The following two photographs feature Weiss and Trifari interpretations of clam brooches.

Antiqued silver-tone clam shell is trimmed with aurora borealis rhinestones and features a single pearl on the inside of the clam shell. The pin is signed ©WEISS on an oval cartouche and measures 2" x 1¾". $50.00 – 75.00.

65

Brooches: Under (and around) the Sea

High quality coral-colored enamel sea shell brooch is trimmed with green enamel seaweed and pearls in a heavy gold-tone setting. The pearls are mounted into the setting. A real beauty, this pin is signed TRIFARI© on a raised rectangle. $50.00 – 75.00.

Unmarked jelly belly fish with blue marquis accents. This pin is similar to design patent number 169172 issued March 31, 1953, to Alfred Philippe (for Trifari). This pin is unsigned so the value is reduced. $35.00 – 60.00. If signed, the value would be much greater.

The starfish is another popular motif. This one features beautifully mounted multicolored rhinestones in an antiqued gold-tone setting with a beautiful swirl design around the edge of the pin. It is signed ART© on a raised rectangle. $50.00 – 75.00.

Brooches: Under (and around) the Sea

Delicate gold-tone starfish features tiny pink rhinestones, faux turquoise cabochons, and seed pearls. A petite pin measuring only 1½" in diameter, it is unsigned. $25.00 – 40.00.

High quality black enamel fish pin has tiny clear rhinestone trim along the fins. Swirling and graceful, the pin measures 2" long. Signed ©PANETTA. $50.00 – 75.00. Panetta jewelry is well made and was expensive relative to other costume jewelry. It is rare in the collectibles market.

Gold-tone fish with faux hematite body and sparkling clear rhinestone eye. The gold setting features lots of interesting detail. The pin measures 1¼" x 1¼". $20.00 – 30.00.

67

Brooches: Under (and around) the Sea

Angel fish has clear rhinestones and red cabochon eye in a gold-tone setting. Notice the touch of green on the bottom of the fins; the pin measures 1½" x 1½" and is signed ©J.J. on a raised rectangle. $25.00 – 40.00.

Mother-of-pearl scales provide an interesting accent in this 3" long gold-tone fish; the setting is very detailed as well. Signed ART© on a raised rectangle. $50.00 – 75.00.

Very well made and surprisingly heavy for a small pin, this dolphin measures just over 1" in length. It features a pretty gold-tone finish with a tiny blue rhinestone eye. Signed GERRY's©. $20.00 – 30.00.

Brooches: Under (and around) the Sea

Unsigned fish features pearl bubble accents. When I purchased this pin it was on a card marked Richelieu but the pin itself is unsigned. There is a lot of interesting detail in the gold-tone setting; the pin measures 1½" x 1¾". $25.00 – 40.00.

This fish brooch features a large faux pearl body in a gold-tone setting. The pin measures almost 2½" from front to back, and over 1" from top to bottom. A real fashion statement! Unsigned. $20.00 – 35.00.

This isn't exactly Botticelli's Venus; this lady has a little attitude! Pretty gold-tone brooch is made in two pieces and measures 2" x 1¼". It is signed Judith Green on a ribbon-shaped cartouche. $35.00 – 60.00.

Brooches: Under (and around) the Sea

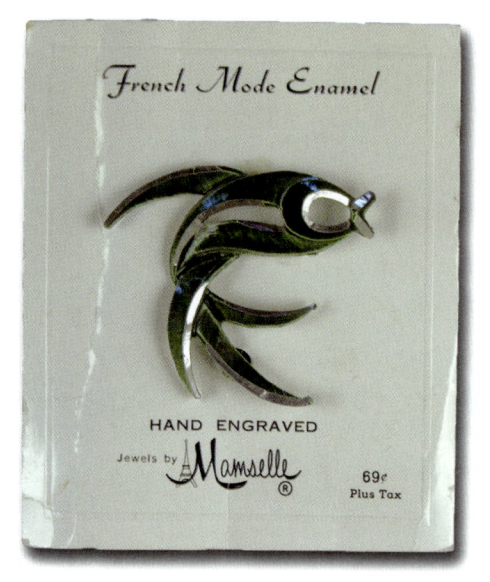

Enamel fish pin is signed ©MAMSELLE in a raised rectangle. The Mamselle signature was first used in 1962; it later appeared with the Eiffel tower symbol in 1968. Mamselle jewelry was made by the Greenberg Company in Providence, Rhode Island, until 1999. This pin is shown on its original card and sold for 69 cents. Over 40 years later, its priced at $10.00 – 20.00.

Enamel swordfish measures 2¼". This pretty enamel pin has glued in aurora borealis rhinestones with green and brown fins and a red rhinestone eye. Remember when folks had these stuffed and hung on their walls? When I was growing up, our neighbor had a large one which I walked by soundlessly lest it notice me. Unsigned. $25.00 – 35.00.

Milk Glass

Top: White glass navettes form an interesting shape in this pin. Also featured are green opaque stones; all are prong-set. The pin measures 2" x 2". Unsigned. $30.00 – 45.00. Middle: Pretty leaf-shaped prongs affix these large pear-shaped milk glass stones in their setting. Unsigned. $30.00 – 45.00. Bottom: Petite and pretty circle pin with marquis-shaped milk glass stones. It measures 1½" in diameter. Unsigned. $20.00 – 35.00.

Brooches: Dangling

Upper left: Half moon design brooch features an overlay of gold strips. This pin is made in two pieces and riveted together. It is signed ©B.S.K. in a raised rectangle. $20.00 – 35.00. Middle: This gigantic swirl of gold-tone measures almost 2½" in diameter. This pin is signed ©MONET. $20.00 – 35.00. Upper right: Swirl pin features a matte gold-tone finish. It still has its original tag that reads on one side "Jewels by Trifari" and shows the crown symbol on the other side. The pin is also marked with the crown TRIFARI© signature. $20.00 – 35.00. Bottom: This gold-tone bar pin is signed NAPIER©. $10.00 – 20.00. This type of gold jewelry is not as collectible as other types of enamel and rhinestone vintage costume jewelry. The prices haven't risen much since these style brooches first made their debut. What I like about them is that they are very wearable, timeless styles and I don't have to worry about losing a rhinestone!

Top: Traditional cameo brooch has pearl accents in an antiqued gold-tone setting. The pin has a bail so it can be worn as a pendant. It measures 1¾" tall x 1½" wide. Signed FLORENZA© on a raised rectangle. $40.00 – 65.00. Bottom: Pearls, golden topaz, and center cameo are featured in this domed silver-tone and white brooch. It measures ¾" deep and 2½" in diameter. Signed FLORENZA© on raised rectangle. $50.00 – 75.00.

Dangling

Left: Oval shaped brooch has a large golden topaz stone in the center, surrounded by a ring of clear rhinestones. The outer rim of the pin has golden topaz alternating with pearls. The three dangling charms pick up the design of the pin's center with golden topaz and clear rhinestone accents. Marked ©Francois, a Coro trademark. $50.00 – 75.00. Middle: Brooch features a large rose cut faux smoky topaz, foiled, in an open back gold-tone setting. The brooch is dotted with tiny golden topaz rhinestones and pearls at the top of the urn design. The entire brooch, including dangling chains measures 3½" from top to bottom. Signed FLORENZA© on raised rectangle. $50.00 – 75.00. Right: A beautiful brooch in antiqued gold-tone setting features red enamel and dangling pearl accents. Clear and red rhinestones provide additional interest. It measures 1½" x 3". Signed ©FLORENZA on a raised rectangle. $50.00 – 75.00.

71

Brooches: Dangling

Top: Faux turquoise stones provide accents for this lovely brooch featuring a large faux mabé pearl in an antiqued gold-tone setting. It has a bail so it can be worn as a pendant. It measures 1½" x 2½" long. Signed FLORENZA© on a raised rectangle. $50.00 – 75.00. Bottom: This brooch features a faux pearl encircled with tiny rhinestones, green cabochons, and pearls. The brooch measures 3" long and has a bail so it can be worn as a pendant. Signed ART©. $50.00 – 75.00.

Alice Caviness was a clothing designer who created jewelry to accent her fashions. Her designs offered a great variety of styles and her hard-to-find jewelry is very collectible. She often used art glass stones and hand-strung beads. This piece features a large center faux turquoise cabochon surrounded by pearls and smaller stones which are all prong-set. The pin measures 4" long including the dangling chains. Signed ALICE CAVINESS on an oval cartouche. $75.00 – 100.00.

Oriental motif brooch has dangling chains with glass and plastic accents and faux jade carvings. Note the dragon and fish motif in the shiny gold-tone setting. This large pin is made in two pieces and measures 2" x 3½" long. Unsigned. $50.00 – 75.00.

72

Brooches: Diamante

Top center: Sara Coventry brooch named "Azure" is accented with faux turquoise cabochons and large center cabochon. It measures 2¼" in diameter. Signed ©SARAH. $30.00 – 45.00. Upper right: Beautiful gold-tone anemone design brooch features turquoise colored cabochons accented with one clear center rhinestone. Signed ©CAPRI on a raised rectangle, this brooch measures just over 2" in diameter. $40.00 – 55.00. Lower right: Petite round domed pin in antiqued gold-tone setting is trimmed with turquoise, green, and blue plastic inserts. The center features a cluster of pink rhinestones. It measures 1½" in diameter and is marked MADE IN GERMANY WEST. $30.00 – 45.00. Lower left: Gold-tone floral spray has turquoise colored beads on moveable stems. The interesting setting has both smooth and textured areas. The brooch measures 2½" long and is signed ©HAR on a raised rectangle. $50.00 – 75.00. Upper left: Gold-tone brooch has turquoise colored cabochons in a snowflake design. This substantial brooch is made in two pieces and riveted together. It measures 2" in diameter. Signed ©AVON. $30.00 – 45.00. In the center, the brooch features a large, prong-set turquoise-colored glass stone in gold-tone setting. The pin is stamped SPINX and also has a four-digit design number next to the signature. $25.00 – 40.00. Spinx is a British firm that was established in 1950. They have made jewelry for Kenneth Jay Lane and Butler and Wilson, among others.

Diamante

Sparkling musical note features clear pavé-set rhinestones. Channel-set baguettes decorate the note's stem in this early example from PELL, a company that is still in business. The pin measures 2" tall and is marked ©PELL. $75.00 – 100.00.

Grand piano pin has clear baguette rhinestones in the keyboard with one askew as originally set. It features a shiny rhodium setting and measures about 2" across. Signed PELL without the copyright symbol. $75.00 – 100.00.

73

Brooches: Diamante

This lovely domed pin sits ¾" high and measures 2" in diameter. A large beauty, it has twenty ½" chaton-cut rhinestones, not to mention the other, smaller stones. This was a gift from my mother and is one of my favorite brooches. Unsigned. $50.00 – 75.00.

Diamante at its best. Left: A truly stunning brooch featuring large, prong-set pear, round, and marquis-shaped rhinestones accented by icing (swirling ribbon design with pavé rhinestones). It measures 2½" at its widest and is signed WEISS with no copyright dating it to before 1955. $100.00 – 125.00. Right: This circle pin is full of lovely prong-set rhinestones, accented by three tiny flowers that are mounted above the main pin. They almost appear to be floating. It is signed WEISS© in an oval cartouche. $75.00 – 100.00.

Left: This large brooch measures 3½" long and features all prong-set rhinestones of many sizes. Note the two flowers with detailed centers. Unsigned. $45.00 – 60.00. Right: This large brooch measures 3" across and has round and marquis-shaped clear stones. A very dimensional pin, it measures ¾" high. Unsigned. $35.00 – 50.00.

BROOCHES: DIAMANTE

Top left: Diamante bow pin is decorated with channel-set baguettes and round rhinestones and is signed HOLLYCRAFT Copr. 1957. $60.00 – 85.00. Top right: Swirling tendrils that seem to float upward have small, clear rhinestones in this lovely brooch by Polcini. An understated and graceful design, it measures 2" at its widest. Signed POLCINI©. $50.00 – 75.00. Originally known as Ledo, Polcini jewelry was made by the Leading Jewelry Manufacturing Company beginning in 1911. Sometime during the early 1960s, the company was renamed Polcini. Known for its pretty designs and high quality materials, both Ledo and Polcini jewelry pieces are rare and very collectible. Lower left: Brooch in silver-tone setting with clear rhinestones, channel-set baguettes form the "vein" through the lower leaf; the center is set off with a pearl accent, signed ©PELL. $75.00 – 100.00. Lower right: Art Deco style brooch is made with clear rhinestones and it is marked WIESNER on an oval cartouche. It measures 1¼" across. $50.00 – 75.00.

Unsigned wine bottle with cocktail glass are scatter pins. The glass is 1¾" high with round, baguette, and pear-shaped rhinestones, all prong-set. Note the pear-shaped rhinestone "dripping" out of the bottle. $35.00 – 50.00.

Left: This large and substantial wreath design brooch is set with clear rhinestones in the base and topped with six flowers done with aurora borealis rhinestones. It measures 2½" in diameter. All stones in the brooch are prong-set in shiny rhodium. $35.00 – 60.00. Right: Prong-set marquis-shaped rhinestones form the base of this lovely brooch; above sit a row of dangling crystals. The flower's stem is loaded with aurora borealis rhinestones. It measures 3½" in length. Unsigned, most likely DeLizza & Elster (Juliana). $50.00 – 75.00.

Brooches: Diamante

Left: Slightly domed brooch has chaton-cut, prong-set sparkling clear rhinestones. The brooch measures ¾" high and 1¾" in diameter. Unsigned. $30.00 – 45.00. Right: Pot-metal dress clip is set with clear marquis-shaped rhinestones and ruby red baguettes, foiled, that are held with pretty prongs. It is marked ATIR0112. The clip measures 2½" high. $50.00 – 75.00.

Left: Diamante cross and orb dates to 1961 – 1962. Right: Diamante cross with anchor dates to 1963 – 1964. These brooches were made for members of the New Jersey Order of the Eastern Star and were available for purchase. Unsigned. $20.00 – 30.00 each.

Top: This diamante brooch in a pot-metal setting reminds me of a butterfly. The pin measures 3" wide and is unmarked. $50.00 – 75.00. Bottom: Long diamante brooch is 5" of pavé leaves and stem alternating with marquis-shaped rhinestones in a rhodium setting. What a fashion statement! $50.00 – 75.00.

Brooches: Butterflies

Butterflies

Regency butterfly in shades of pink features various shaped, prong-set rhinestones. Collectors consider Regency butterflies to be among the best ever made. It is easy to see why from this lovely example. Signed REGENCY on an oval cartouche. $100.00 – 125.00.

Beautiful cream colored enameled floral brooch features a delicate rhinestone and pearl trimmed trembler butterfly. Signed ART©. $75.00 – 100.00.

Pair of moths with large turquoise plastic cabochons and pearl accents in gold-tone setting. Signed ©B.S.K. $40.00 – 65.00 pair.

77

Brooches: Butterflies

Left: Butterfly has prong-set smooth and faceted stones. Unsigned. $20.00 – 30.00. Right: Butterfly has smooth opalescent stones and red cabochons with tiny rhinestones; all but the center cabs are prong-set. Signed ©Hobé. $40.00 – 65.00.

Left: Antiqued gold-tone butterfly has enamel trim and white plastic pear-shaped stones. It measures 1¾" across. Signed CENO©. $25.00 – 40.00. Right: Stylized butterfly with brightly colored rhinestones signed EISENBERG ICE©. $50.00 – 75.00.

Left: Golden moth with ruby red prong-set stones signed CZECH on an oval cartouche. $50.00 – 75.00. Right: Golden topaz rhinestones decorate the edge of this sunny butterfly brooch that also features frosted marquis stones. It measures 2" x 2½" and is marked WEISS on an oval cartouche. $75.00 – 90.00.

Brooches: Purples

Purples

Top left: Pearl and aurora borealis rhinestones are featured in this pretty pin in the shape of a bush. It is signed Francois on a raised rectangle. $50.00 – 75.00. Top right: Purple, red, and aurora borealis rhinestones are featured in a rose gold-tone setting; all stones are prong-set. It is a very lightweight brooch measuring 2½" x 3". Unsigned. $40.00 – 65.00. Lower left: Brooch features three aurora borealis flowers with dangling pale lavender stones. It measures 2¾" long. Unsigned. $40.00 – 65.00. Lower right: Pretty iridescent stones are featured in this brooch with various sizes of stones including a large center cabochon. Unsigned. $40.00 – 65.00.

Large brooch measures 3" across x 1" high. This unsigned cushion design pin features multicolored stones including green, black, purple, and pink in a gold-tone setting. $75.00 – 100.00.

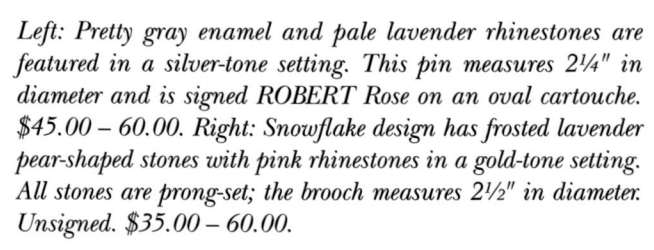

Left: Pretty gray enamel and pale lavender rhinestones are featured in a silver-tone setting. This pin measures 2¼" in diameter and is signed ROBERT Rose on an oval cartouche. $45.00 – 60.00. Right: Snowflake design has frosted lavender pear-shaped stones with pink rhinestones in a gold-tone setting. All stones are prong-set; the brooch measures 2½" in diameter. Unsigned. $35.00 – 60.00.

Brooches: Purples

Upper left: Purple rhinestones are accents in this pretty gold-tone setting with leaves. Signed LISNER©. $35.00 – 60.00. Upper right: Faceted stones in pale lavender with open backs reflect the light in interesting ways. Large center stone with open back measures 1" in diameter; the brooch itself measures 2" in diameter. All stones are prong-set, possibly DeLizza and Elster (Juliana). $50.00 – 75.00. Lower left: Beautiful dress clip has pale lavender rhinestones. This was a gift from my sister and brother-in-law. The design reminds me of a bunch of grapes. Unsigned. $40.00 – 65.00. Lower right: Red stones provide a pretty contrast in this otherwise purple and pink brooch. It is dominated by a large center, unfoiled stone which measures ¾". Overall, this petite pin measures 1" x 1½". Unsigned. $30.00 – 45.00.

Retro Modern Style

Upper left: Gold-tone brooch has purple prong-set stones. It is stamped Coro in one place and signed again on a raised rectangle with the Pegasus symbol and Coro signature and STERLING. $125.00 – 150.00. Upper right: Floral spray has pink prong-set rhinestones and pearl centers in the flowers. Note the clear rhinestone trim. It is stamped STERLING. $75.00 – 100.00. Bottom: Yellow and rose gold floral spray has a center blue stone and is signed REGEL and 1/20 12K. $75.00 – 100.00.

Top left: Large brooch on left matches exactly design patent #136,868 filed September 17, 1943, by A. Katz (Figure 18). It measures 4½" high and is marked Coro STERLING. $125.00 – 150.00. Top right: Yellow and rose gold floral spray with amethyst colored, prong-set stones. Signed 1/20 10K in circle with a capital H overlaid with a capital "I" which is the mark of Harry Iskin. $75.00 – 100.00. Lower right: Bow brooch in yellow and rose gold finish with channel-set red baguettes and clear stones. It measures 3" across and is marked TAYLORD 1/20 12K GOLDFILLED. $75.00 – 100.00.

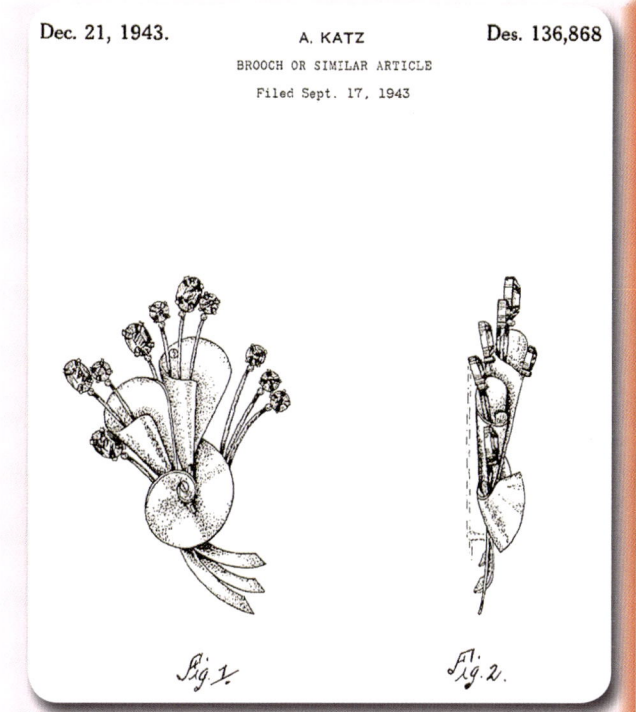

Brooches: Retro Modern Style

Dec. 21, 1943.   A. KATZ   **Des. 136,868**
BROOCH OR SIMILAR ARTICLE
Filed Sept. 17, 1943

Figure 18. Copy of A. Katz patent for brooch or similar article

Upper right: The large brooch is made in three pieces and features a huge garnet colored prong-set stone. Unsigned. $75.00 – 100.00. Lower left: Petite and pretty, this small brooch features clear and amethyst stones in an interesting gold-tone setting. Unsigned. $25.00 – 40.00.

Left: Calvaire Sterling brooch measures 4" tall, and features red and clear stones, prong-set, with very detailed metal work. Calvaire jewelry is extremely rare. CALVAIRE and STERLING are imprinted in the metal. $275.00 – 325.00. Right: Brooch in striking deco design featuring clear and pink stones and very detailed metal work. Unsigned. $75.00 – 100.00.

Brooches: Retro Modern Style

Lovely gold-tone brooch has large center faux turquoise cabochon surrounded by tiny pearls and a row of turquoise cabochons along the bottom of the brooch. It is signed Coro in script with no copyright symbol. This pin matches design patent #147,190 issued on July 22, 1947, to A. Katz (see Figure 19). $75.00 – 100.00.

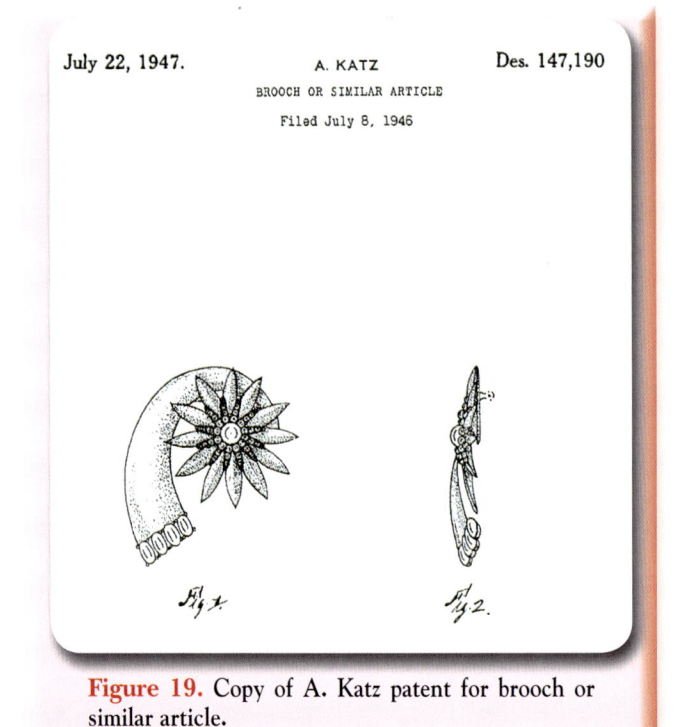

Figure 19. Copy of A. Katz patent for brooch or similar article.

Miscellaneous

Upper left: Three pieces of copper combine in a modernist design. This shiny copper brooch measures 1¾" x 2" and is signed Coro with the Pegasus symbol on two of three pieces. $25.00 – 50.00. Upper right: Pretty geometric brooch in matte silver-tone and copper measures 3" x 1½". The pattern in the copper reminds me of an animal print. Signed ©MONET on a raised rectangle. $25.00 – 50.00. Bottom: Copper and enameled leaf brooch. The green enamel is almost iridescent. This brooch is made in four pieces! Measuring almost 2" x 3½", the brooch is signed MATISSE ©RENOIR. $50.00 – 75.00.

Brooches: Miscellaneous

Top: Silver-tone floral bouquet in a basket has enamel, moonstones, and clear rhinestone accents in a pot-metal setting. Unsigned. $50.00 – 75.00. Lower right: Brooch by Sarah Coventry is named Wisteria from spring 1962. It features purple and pink rhinestones in a silver-tone setting and measures 2" x 3". Signed ©SARAHCOV on a raised rectangle. $30.00 – 55.00. Lower left: Silver-tone spray is accented with small berries. The pin measures 1¾" x 2½" and is signed ©LISNER. $20.00 – 35.00.

Top left: Graceful, elongated hand has fire engine red fingernails, a large "diamond" ring flanked by four smaller rhinestones, and a matching bracelet. This brooch is very similar in design to design patent #139,075 granted October 10, 1944, to A. Katz (see Figure 20). However, the brooch in the photograph is unsigned. It measures almost 2½" long. $25.00 – 50.00. Lower right: The smaller gold-tone brooch shows a delicate hand holding a prong-set pearl. A faint elevation of the fourth finger provides the suggestion of a ring. Measuring a little over 1¼", the pin is unsigned. $20.00 – 35.00.

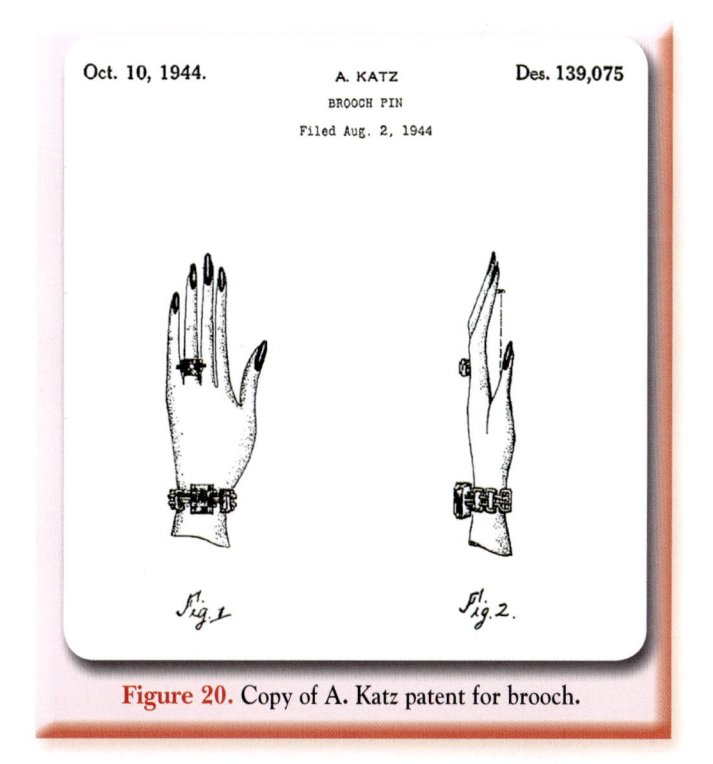

Figure 20. Copy of A. Katz patent for brooch.

Brooches: Miscellaneous

Upper left: Clear rhinestones accent the tips of the branches for a gorgeous effect on this colorful Christmas tree pin. Signed CASTLECLIFF. $45.00 – 60.00. *Upper middle:* Shiny gold-tone Christmas tree has symmetrically placed rhinestones. Signed ©J.J. on a raised rectangle. $25.00 – 40.00. *Upper right:* Colorful rhinestones decorate a snazzy, stylized gold-tone Christmas tree. Unsigned. $25.00 – 50.00. *Lower left:* Enameled tree has a colorful garland set has rhinestones. Signed ©ART. $35.00 – 60.00. *Lower middle:* Delicate and dimensional Christmas tree with various stones including opaque faux turquoise. This is a petite pin and measures just 1¾" tall. Signed ©BOUCHER. $45.00 – 60.00. *Lower right:* Deep green enameled Christmas tree brooch is made in two pieces and riveted together. Signed ©ART. $35.00 – 60.00.

Upper left: Christmas dove with rhinestone and enameled accents signed ©MYLU. $35.00 – 60.00. *Upper middle:* Christmas candle with red plastic berries and enameled accents. Signed ©ROMA. $25.00 – 50.00. *Upper right:* Christmas bell brooch with red and green rhinestones has channel-set baguette trim. Signed ©PELL. $45.00 – 60.00. *Lower left:* Christmas pooch has red rhinestone eyes and Santa cap. Signed GERRY'S©. $15.00 – 25.00. *Lower right:* Pretty Christmas kitty is unsigned. $10.00 – 15.00.

Browns and Blacks

Left: Oval brooch in antiqued gold-tone features a star pattern and pearl trim. Unsigned. $30.00 – 55.00. *Right:* Dramatic black center starburst design is prong-set in an elaborate antiqued setting. Tiny black chatons provide additional accents. Signed ©FLORENZA. $50.00 – 75.00.

Brooches: Browns and Blacks

Lower left: Bright orange cabochons are featured in this ornate, domed gold-tone brooch. It measures ¾" deep x 2" long x 1¾" wide. Small burnt orange cabochons add dimension and interest. Signed ©HAR. $60.00 – 85.00. *Middle:* Brightly colored pear-shaped and plastic cabochons are featured in an antiqued gold-tone setting. Brooch has a bail so it can be worn as a pendant. It measures 2½" in diameter and is signed SELINI© on a raised rectangle. $50.00 – 75.00. *Upper right:* Sarah Coventry brooch is named Tangerine and dates from 1973. It features a gold-tone openwork design with small plastic cabochons. The pin measures 2" x 2½" wide. I purchased the pin in its original package, which described it as a hostess gift. Signed ©SARAH. $25.00 – 40.00.

Lower left: Lightweight free form brooch has prong-set black stones. Unsigned. $40.00 – 65.00. *Upper right:* Dimensional, domed brooch measures 1" high x 2½" across. It features all prong-set black stones. Unsigned. $30.00 – 55.00.

Left: Brooch in gold-tone filigree setting features a large hematite center cabochon encircled with pearls and black diamonds. The pin measures 1¾" in diameter. Unsigned. $25.00 – 50.00. *Right:* Cameo set on black glass background has an antiqued gold-tone setting. It measures 1½" x 1¼". Unsigned. $35.00 – 60.00.

Brooches: Browns and Blacks

Top: Large domed brooch in antiqued gold-tone setting features alternating rows of gold-tone swirls and brown prong-set rhinestones. The large center cabochon is plastic. Signed HAR©. $50.00 – 75.00. Bottom: Spectacular brooch with intaglio center shows cupid trying to retrieve his arrow. Each prong emanating from the center features detailed charms including plastic cameo, fly, snake, flower, butterfly, and a crown among others. Beautifully detailed but unsigned, most likely Goldette. $100.00 – 125.00.

Antiqued silver-tone star design has black accents and clear rhinestones. The pin measures 2" in diameter. The star pattern is repeated in the center of the brooch. Brooch signed FLORENZA© on a raised rectangle. $50.00 – 75.00.

Top: Molten textured stones and pretty brown, cognac colored, and aurora borealis prong-set stones are featured in this brooch. Signed REGENCY on oval cartouche. $60.00 – 85.00. Bottom: Lightweight gold-tone is the setting for this pretty brooch. It has aurora borealis, brown and black diamond rhinestones, and measures 3" across. Unsigned. $60.00 – 85.00.

Brooches: Fruits

Fruits

Top left: Antiqued white setting has both fruit and flowers. The flowers have pearl centers trimmed with aurora borealis rhinestones. The fruit is wired to the brooch; overall it measures 2½" x 2½". Signed ©HAR on a raised rectangle. $50.00 – 75.00. Bottom right: Realistic-looking bananas and flowers make up this fun brooch. The pin measures 2" x 2". Signed SELINI©. $50.00 – 75.00.

Left: Beautiful enameled apple has delicate clear rhinestone trim on the leaf. This pin measures 2" x 1½". Signed ©HAR. $35.00 – 60.00. Right: Enameled strawberry with textured surface. Signed B.S.K. $25.00 – 50.00.

Double strawberry pin has red and green rhinestones in a japanned setting. This petite pin measures just 1½" across x 1" tall. Signed WEISS on an oval cartouche. $35.00 – 60.00.

87

Brooches: Fruits

Upper left: Simply gorgeous aurora borealis rhinestone pin is in the shape of a pear. Unsigned. $35.00 – 60.00. Upper right: Frosted fruit pin is signed ©SARAHCOV. It measures just 1¾" x 1¾". $20.00 – 35.00. Bottom: Detailed and well made gold-tone fruit cluster pin has clear rhinestone accents. The fruits are wired to the pin back. Signed ©Coro. $30.00 – 55.00.

Shiny gold-tone and clear rhinestones trim this dramatic strawberry brooch that reminds me of a Boucher design. However, it is signed ©Coro. $50.00 – 75.00.

Enameled avocado design brooch signed Coro. $25.00 – 50.00.

Brooches: Armour

Armour

Dagger and scabbard with black enamel, turquoise, and coral colored opaque stones is trimmed in clear rhinestones. The dagger can be worn in its scabbard or chatelaine style. A beautiful piece, unsigned. $125.00 – 150.00.

The dagger is shown out of its scabbard in this photo.

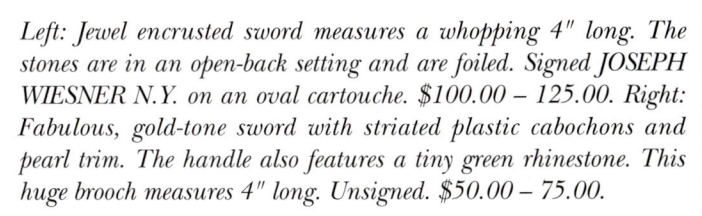

Left: Jewel encrusted sword measures a whopping 4" long. The stones are in an open-back setting and are foiled. Signed JOSEPH WIESNER N.Y. on an oval cartouche. $100.00 – 125.00. Right: Fabulous, gold-tone sword with striated plastic cabochons and pearl trim. The handle also features a tiny green rhinestone. This huge brooch measures 4" long. Unsigned. $50.00 – 75.00.

89

Brooches, Armour

Left: Diamante brooch in rhodium setting is marked on an oval cartouche KRAMER. PAT. PEND. $60.00 – 85.00. Middle: Diamante sword with crown TRIFARI signature measures 2¾" long. $60.00 – 85.00. Right: Antiqued silver-tone pin features a faux turquoise stone. The metal has a very detailed pattern on both sides of the pin. Stamped MIRACLE. $35.00 – 60.00.

Thermoplastic face is set in matte gold-tone with clear rhinestone and chain accents. This fabulous pin measures over 2" high x 1½" wide. It is signed SELRO CORP. on a raised rectangle. This type of face jewelry by SELRO is highly collectible. $100.00 – 125.00.

Top left: Colorful gladiator helmet has pearl trim and is richly detailed. Signed ©ART. $50.00 – 75.00. Lower right: Heraldic brooch in antiqued gold-tone setting features enameled royal crest in red and blue. It has a bail so it can be worn as a pendant. It measures 2½" high x 2" wide. Signed Reinad 5th AV, N.Y. $75.00 – 100.00.

Brooches: Faces

Faces

Large gold-tone Asian princess trimmed with clear and ruby red rhinestones. This is a popular design made by Reinad with many slight variations. Unsigned. $125.00 – 175.00.

Lower left: Older Blackamoor brooch features rhinestone accents and elaborate headdress. There is some enamel loss on this pin. It measures 2¾" high. Unsigned. $75.00 – 100.00. Middle: Shiny red and black enameled figure has an ornate turban and harem pants with rhinestone trim. The brooch measures 3" high including the tall feather on the turban. Signed ART© on raised rectangle. $75.00 – 100.00. Upper right: Genie with a turban and crystal ball features the kind of detail collectors associate with HAR. This piece is a charm or small pendant. Signed ©HAR. $75.00 – 100.00.

Blackamoor chatelaine with enameled faces and clear rhinestone eyes. Blackamoor jewelry was popular in the 1930s. The clear rhinestone eyes are a replacement. Unsigned. $20.00 – 45.00.

91

Brooches: Faces

Left: Elegant and regal Blackamoor brooch with beautiful jeweled outfit is accented with tiny colored and clear rhinestones in a gold-tone setting. It measures 2¼" high x 1½" wide. This is a beautiful piece, signed BUTLER on a raised rectangle. $75.00 – 100.00. Right: Blackamoor princess with elaborate headdress and finally detailed earrings. Measures 2" high x 1¼" at widest. Unsigned. $50.00 – 75.00.

This style face brooch is often described as Elzac. In her book entitled Costume & Figural Jewelry, *author Kathy Flood notes that turquoise ceramic faces backed with patterned copper such as this pin are not Elzac. Nevertheless, it is an interesting brooch with lots of character. Unsigned. $25.00 – 40.00.*

Elzac ceramic and red Lucite bonnet head face pin matches design patent #135,101 issued on February 23, 1943, to Elliot Handler (Figure 21). $175.00 – 225.00.

92

Brooches: Animals

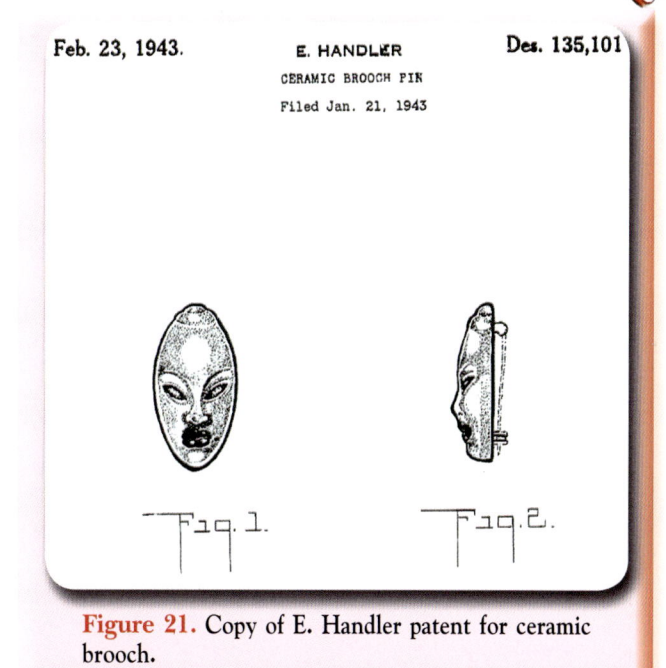

Figure 21. Copy of E. Handler patent for ceramic brooch.

Elzac "Victim of Fashion" brooch measures a whopping 4½" long. The ceramic face is topped with an elaborate felt headdress which is accented with a pearl. Elzac pieces are becoming increasingly popular among collectors. $175.00 – 225.00.

Animals

This massive and heavy brooch was designed by Elizabeth Taylor's daughter, Liza Todd Tivey, and bears her initials on the right front. Liza Todd is an accomplished sculptress as evidenced by the beautifully rendered horse heads. The brooch measures 2⅞" x 2⅞" and is marked ELIZABETH TAYLOR and AVON with a center E in script on an oval cartouche. $100.00 – 125.00.

93

Brooches: Animals

Top: Beautiful leopard brooch feautres a cat crouching on a branch and ready to pounce. Marked ©FLORENZA on a raised rectangle, it measures 1½" long. $50.00 – 75.00. Bottom: Gorgeous leopard has pavé set rhinestones and black stone accents. Signed RICHELIEU on a raised rectangle. $50.00 – 75.00.

Left: Large figural pin measures almost 4" tall. The rooster is marked JEANNE and is trimmed with red and clear rhinestones. Jeanne is an unusual mark; while little is known about this company, the pieces that do appear in the collectibles market are high quality. $50.00 – 75.00. Right: Petite chick is shown emerging from its shell. It has a gold-tone finish with a smooth red rhinestone eye and is signed with the crown TRIFARI© signature on a raised rectangle. The pin is made in two pieces and riveted together. $35.00 – 60.00.

Elephant brooch features coral, burgundy, and mustard-colored plastic inserts. Faux ivory tusks and toenails add additional detail to this wonderful figural brooch. Signed Hattie Carnegie on an oval cartouche. $175.00 – 225.00.

Brooches: Animals

Top: Heavy fox brooch is set with pavé rhinestones and green cabochon eyes. A very dimensional pin, it is ¾" high. Unsigned. $30.00 – 55.00. Left: Bunny brooch features a large iridescent cabochon belly. Pretty pink rhinestones provide additional accents. It is signed PELL©. $35.00 – 60.00. Right: Enameled skunks have dramatic diamante trim. This is a very dimensional and heavy pin and is made in two pieces. Signed A&S (for Atwood and Sawyer, a British company founded in 1956). $35.00 – 60.00.

Elzac style ceramic bunny brooch has Lucite ears and tail. Elzac pieces were identified by tags so the items themselves are not marked. $125.00 – 150.00.

Beautiful blue enameled ram's head brooch features a rhinestone eye, jeweled collar, and beautifully detailed curved horns. This is a very heavy and well made piece. Signed Richelieu on a raised rectangle. $50.00 – 75.00.

Brooches: Animals

Besides their fantastic enameled figures of dragons, cobras, and genies, HAR also made smaller, more whimsical pieces such as this funny monkey with blue rhinestone eyes and trim. Caught in mid-stride, he measures just 1¾" high. Signed ©HAR. $50.00 – 75.00.

Antiqued gold-tone snakes are coiled around a white plastic cabochon egg. The brooch is signed ART©. $60.00 – 85.00.

Left: High quality, heavy black enamel brooch with gold-tone accents. Both have tiny blue eyes. Unsigned. $25.00 – 35.00. Right: Cute black and white Scotties pin. Unsigned. $25.00 – 35.00.

Brooches: People

Top center: Poodle pin has coral colored plastic scarab insets on legs and head. Unsigned. $20.00 – 30.00. Upper right: Yorkshire terrier has clear rhinestone accents and green coat. Unsigned. $20.00 – 30.00. Lower right: Aurora borealis stones almost completely cover the surface of this pretty poodle. Unsigned. $30.00 – 45.00. Lower left: Time for a stretch. This pretty gold-tone poodle has quite a haircut. Note the red rhinestone eyes and detailed facial expression. Signed MONET©. $35.00 – 50.00. Upper left: Delicate dachshund brooch with very detailed face and clear rhinestone accents. Signed BOUCHER and DACHSHUND and 7913 (an inventory number) each in its own raised rectangle. $50.00 – 75.00.

Silver dragon brooch is stamped MEXICO 925 and 7H – 7B. This graceful design has a bail so it can be worn as a pendant. Measuring 1½" x 2", the smooth surface of this lightweight brooch seems to shimmer. $75.00 – 100.00.

People

Male and female figural brooches of Asian design have clear rhinestone trim and pearl faces in an antiqued gold-tone setting. They each measure 2¼" high. Notice the detail in the garment and headdress. Remarkably, these brooches are unsigned but they remind me of figural brooches by Nettie Rosenstein. $75.00 – 100.00 for the pair.

Brooches: People

Left: Faux jade Buddha is held in place by prongs. The back of the ornate setting in which the figure sits features Chinese characters. Unsigned. $35.00 – 60.00. Right: Asian figure has flowing robes, plastic marbled cabochon belly, and rust colored plastic cabochon for the face. The brooch measures 1¾" tall. Signed MARVELLA©. $50.00 – 75.00.

Very detailed enameled brooch features a pirate with a leg on his booty. The paint has seen better days but jewelry with the Halbe mark is rare and their jewelry was high quality. This piece is signed HALBE and also has an E etched into the metal. The company was in business from the 1950s to 1960s. $50.00 – 75.00.

Left: Gold-tone water carrier with rhinestone accents. It is signed CORO with the Pegasus symbol. $50.00 – 75.00. Right: Very detailed, beautifully rendered brooch features clear rhinestone trim on the bottom of the man's robe and at the tip of his hat, edge of his sleeve, and around the lantern. Note the dragon design on the lantern. Unsigned. $50.00 – 75.00.

Brooches: Pearls

Pearls

Brooch featuring a large center faux jade stone in Miriam Haskell's signature gold filigree setting, surrounded with tiny seed pearls. Collectors agree that Miriam Haskell jewelry is among the finest costume jewelry ever made. This brooch measures 2" x 2½" and is signed MIRIAM HASKELL on an oval cartouche. $200.00 – 250.00.

Outstanding brooch with three large dangling pearls and a large pumpkin-colored cabochon. Clear rhinestones provide additional accents in this dramatic pin. Signed HATTIE CARNEGIE on an oval cartouche. $150.00 – 175.00.

Left: Gold-tone tree is laden with luscious pearls. Signed MARVELLA© on a raised cartouche. $50.00 – 75.00. Right: Some of the fruit from the tree has found its way into this gold-tone wheelbarrow brooch. Unsigned. $20.00 – 35.00.

Brooches: Pearls

Upper left: Brooch featuring a bunch of grapes with gold-tone accents. The graceful leaves are very detailed. This is a petite pin measuring just 1" x 1½". Signed ROMA©. $25.00 – 50.00. Upper right: Dozens of tiny clear rhinestones in a gold-tone setting make this a lovely brooch. A large center faux pearl provides a beautiful accent. Unsigned. $25.00 – 50.00. Lower left: Heavy fan-shaped brooch is made in two pieces. It features pearls and clear rhinestones and is signed ©HAR on a raised rectangle. $100.00 – 125.00. Lower right: Seed pearls are featured in a matte and shiny gold-tone setting. This large brooch measures over 2" x 2" at its widest and is made in two pieces. Signed ©B.S.K. $35.00 – 60.00.

Outstanding Weiss brooch features gold-tone roses, opalescent stones, and pearls which are prong-set. This graceful and elegant brooch measures just over 2¼" by 2¼". There is some foil loss on the rhinestones. It is signed WEISS on an oval cartouche. $75.00 – 100.00.

Earthtones

Upper left: Gorgeous rose cut tourmalines are the focal point of this pretty brooch. Cognac colored and green rhinestones add additional accents. All stones are prong-set; the outer stones have open backs. It measures 2½" x 2" and is unsigned. $50.00 – 75.00. Upper right: Beautiful brown, golden topaz, green, and rust colored rhinestones accent this layered circular brooch. It is signed EMMONS© on a raised rectangle. $25.00 – 50.00. Bottom: Perennially popular bow design pin features golden topaz, citrine, and cognac colored rhinestones with red stone accents in an antiqued gold-tone setting. It measures 2½" x 2" and is signed ©WEISS. $50.00 – 75.00.

100

Brooches: Bugs and Critters

Upper left: This Sarah Coventry piece was named Acapulco and dates to 1969. A matching bracelet and earrings were also available for purchase. Signed ©SARAHCOV. $20.00 – 45.00. Upper right: Gold-tone pin has golden topaz, citrine colored, and opalescent marquis-shaped stones in a pretty swirl design. Signed ©ART. $30.00 – 55.00. Lower center: Yellow and golden topaz colored cabochons accent the large center stone in this lovely pin. Aurora borealis rhinestones encircle the center stone and provide additional, pretty detail. Unsigned possibly DeLizza and Elster (Juliana). $50.00 – 75.00.

Lower left: Beautiful cognac colored rose cut cabochons are featured in this lovely star design pin. Marquis-shaped iridescent stones provide accents. All of the stones are prong-set. The brooch measures 3" in diameter. Unsigned. $25.00 – 50.00. Middle: Double circle pin has alternating aurora borealis and moonstones in one ring; the other ring features a row of aurora borealis stones next to a row of moonstones. All are prong-set. The pin measures 1½" x 1¾" and is unsigned. $25.00 – 50.00. Right: This dramatic pin features pearlized stones and citrine and golden topaz colored rhinestones. All of the stones, except those encircling the center stone, are prong-set. This beautiful brooch measures 2½" in diameter. Unsigned. $50.00 – 75.00.

Bugs and Critters

Top center: White and black enameled beetle brooch is signed WEISS. $35.00 – 60.00. Top right: Black plastic cabochon is covered by pearl-encrusted wings with black accents. This stylized ladybug with pearl face and green eyes is signed Hattie Carnegie© on an oval cartouche. $45.00 – 70.00. Lower right: Peach plastic bug with gold-tone accents is unsigned. It measures 1½" long; the small gold-tone stones are set into the plastic and the pin is made in two pieces. $25.00 – 50.00. Center bottom: Fly pin has a large center marquis and channel-set baguettes with clear rhinestone trim in a rhodium setting. Pin measures just over 1" x 1¾". Signed ©PELL. $25.00 – 50.00. Lower left: Petite peach-colored plastic beetle in gold-tone setting. Unsigned. $20.00 –$35.00. Upper left: Tiny bug with black enameled body and head measures just 1" long. The wings are encrusted with green and clear rhinestones. Unsigned. $25.00 – 40.00.

101

Brooches: Bugs and Critters

Left: Shiny gold-tone is the setting for this bug with trembler wings. Trimmed with green and clear rhinestones, it measures 1½" long. Signed JEANNE© on an oval cartouche. $50.00 – 75.00. Right: Clear rhinestones in a shiny gold-tone setting are featured in this brooch; when the wearer moves, the wings tremble. Very lifelike movement signed Hattie Carnegie on an oval cartouche. $75.00 – 100.00.

Huge spider brooch in japanned setting measures almost 3½" across. It features large golden topaz-colored stones. The large pear-cut center stone and chaton-cut head rhinestones are unfoiled. All are prong-set. The opaque stones in the spider legs are prong-set. It is signed on an oval cartouche KENNETH LANE©. $50.00 – 75.00.

Demi Parures and Parures

This rich gold-tone set features very large clear rhinestones set into the skin of the fruit. The fruit itself is prong-set; the vines you see are holding it in place. The pin measures 2½" from top to bottom and is marked on an oval cartouche DE NICOLA. One earring is also marked. $75.00 – 100.00.

Demi Parures and Parures

Gold-tone flower brooch with ribbon design has matching earrings. The pin measures just over 2" in diameter. Both shiny and matte finishes provide interest and texture. Each earring is signed Coro on the screwback mechanism. The brooch is signed with the Pegasus symbol followed by Coro©. $35.00 – 60.00.

This large brooch and matching gold-tone earrings are from Trifari's Star Ray line and were featured in their 1966 fall/winter catalog; the set was also made in silver-tone. It is a large pin, measuring over 3" in diameter and is made in two pieces. It is signed with the crown TRIFARI© on a raised rectangle. The earrings measure 1" and are stamped TRIFARI. $50.00 – 75.00.

Beautiful and striking half moon textured gold-tone brooch with large and small pastel colored rhinestones is dotted with tiny turquoise stones. The brooch is 2¾" at the longest point. Some of the rhinestones have open backs and are foiled. The clip back earrings measure 1". This set has the look of La Roco. When La Roco sets are signed, it is usually only the earrings. Unsigned. $60.00 – 85.00.

Demi Parures and Parures

Sarah Coventry four-piece set named Remembrance includes pin with bail, matching clip earrings, and the less common stickpin. The brooch is signed in a raised rectangle ©SARAHCOV and measures 2¾" long x 2½" wide. The stickpin is signed ©SARAHCOV stamped in the metal; and each earring is similarly marked in two places including on the earring clip and on a raised rectangle. $35.00 – 60.00.

Pretty and ornate antiqued gold-tone brooch features a crown motif at the top and large faux turquoise as the centerpiece. The pin, including fringe, measures just over 2½" in length and 1½" wide. The matching clip earrings and brooch are all signed FLORENZA© on raised rectangles. $50.00 – 75.00.

Sarah Coventry Maharani brooch and clip earrings are favorites among collectors and are often featured in vintage costume jewelry books. Here is how the set is described in a July 1969 ad from McCall's magazine: "elegant jewelry for the woman who dares to be different…'Maharani' dazzles as a prodigious pin, pendant, or gala evening ensemble. Specially designed for our 20th anniversary, this fabulous creation combines marquise stones, polished turquoise beads, and imported rhinestones in a shameless display of Sarah's fashion wizardry." This lovely pin and matching earrings feature faux turquoise cabochons accented with emerald green and clear rhinestones in a stunning combination of color. The brooch is signed ©SARAHCOV on raised rectangle; the earrings are signed similarly on the clip mechanism. $50.00 – 75.00.

Demi Parures and Parures

Heart-shaped matte gold-tone and enameled brooch with faux opal center stone, pavé rhinestones, and pearl accents measures 2½" at its widest. The lovely matching earrings are similar in design. This set was named Heart of Hollywood. All pieces are signed on an oval cartouche ELIZABETH TAYLOR across the top; AVON across the bottom, and a capital E in script between the two. Ms. Taylor designed jewelry for Avon from 1993 to 1997. $125.00 – 150.00.

Avon set from 1993 by José Maria Barrera is named Roman Holiday. This demi features a large (3¾") domed brooch with "Trevi fountain" blue enamel in gold-tone set off by a large pearl in the center. This heavy piece can also be worn as a pendant. The matching earrings are very substantial as well. Because this jewelry was sold more recently, collectors can often find them with their original packaging. $75.00 – 100.00.

Elizabeth Taylor for Avon demi parure is named Sea Shimmer. The accompanying brochure describes this lovely set as follows: "With gracefully flowing fins and glowing opalescent scales, these shimmering gold-tone fish breath out bubbles of faux pearls. The ear clips curl delicately around the ears as though somersaulting through a wave. The impressive pin features two rhinestone-sparked fish intertwined in pursuit of a brilliant faux sapphire." Ms. Taylor's jewelry for Avon came packaged in purple felt pouches. The pin measures almost 4½" long x 2" wide. It is signed on an oval cartouche ELIZABETH TAYLOR across the top; AVON across the bottom and a E between the two. $125.00 – 150.00.

Demi Parures and Parures

Sarah Coventry set named Blue Lagoon is from 1964. This is one of the most popular and collectible of all Sarah Coventry sets. Three rows of pretty prong-set blue and aurora borealis rhinestones are featured in an elongated oval shape in a shiny rhodium setting. The brooch measures 2½" long and the matching clip earrings measure 1" from top to bottom. Signed SARAHCOV© on the brooch; the earrings are similarly signed and include PAT. PEND. This set was made by DeLizza and Elster for Sarah Coventry. $75.00 – 100.00.

Dimensional heart-shaped brooch has matching clip earrings. The brooch features a large, heart shaped foiled rhinestone in center. This beautifully made brooch is marked Capri©. The earrings are similarly signed. Capri jewelry was produced from 1952 to 1977; jewelry without the copyright symbol was made between 1952 and 1955. $150.00 – 175.00.

Demi featuring emerald green rhinestones, all prong-set, in a shiny gold-tone setting. The Lucite cameo has been applied to the glass background. The matching clip style earrings are similarly made. The brooch measures almost 2½" x 2" wide. Unsigned. $75.00 – 100.00.

Demi Parures and Parures

Alternating clear and frosted blue rhinestones are prong-set in pretty silver-tone. Note the matching clip earrings are as large as the brooch and measure 2" in length. Unsigned. $50.00 – 75.00.

Gorgeous large brooch measuring 3" wide features tourmaline, emerald green, pale green, and blue prong-set rhinestones. The paperweight stones are smooth, pear shaped, and large — they each measure ¾" long! There are two in the brooch and one in each clip style earring. The set is unsigned. $75.00 – 100.00.

Blue on blue brooch has matching clip earrings. The pin measures 3½" long and the earrings measure 1" long. Weiss often made sets like this but this one is unsigned. $35.00 – 60.00.

Demi Parures and Parures

Ciner creamy white enameled pin with matching clip earrings feature tiny clear rhinestones that run the length of the graceful brooch and earrings. The pin measures 2¼" in length; the earrings measure 1¼" long. Ciner made high quality costume jewelry beginning in the early 1930s. Prior to that they made expensive fine jewelry. Their designs are noted for rows of tiny stones and excellent gold-plated metal work. The pin is marked CINER on the stem of the brooch; both earrings are also signed CINER on the clip backs; there is a patent number PAT156452 issued on December 13, 1949, for the earring clip finding. $100.00 – 125.00.

This brooch features shades of blue rhinestones with matching clip earrings in a rhodium setting. Large givre stones are the focal points of the brooch and earrings. Probably DeLizza and Elster (Juliana). Unsigned. $100.00 – 125.00.

Left: Silver-tone brooch with lovely prong-set blue and green rhinestones with clear rhinestones accents. The large dangling pear-shaped stone is almost ¾" long; the brooch measures 3¼" overall. Clip back earrings are marked in two places; they are stamped AUSTRIA on the earring backs and on top of the earring clips on a round cartouche. The brooch is stamped AUSTRIA as well. $100.00 – 125.00. Right: Beautiful brooch in shiny rhodium setting has open back stones which are all prong-set, including the small green rhinestones. The pin measures a full 3" long and features matching clip earrings. Unsigned. $100.00 – 125.00.

Demi Parures and Parures

Beautiful rhinestone demi features clear blue and aurora borealis rhinestones, all prong-set in a silver-tone setting. The stones that encircle the center stone are mounted on an angle to achieve a pretty floral effect. The brooch measures 1½" in diameter. The matching clip earrings are similarly set, measure ¾" in diameter, and are stamped WEISS. $75.00 – 100.00.

Faux turquoise stones in a substantial, matte gold-tone, fan-shaped setting make up this beautiful brooch. I purchased the brooch with the earrings shown but they are not a set. The brooch is 2¼" wide x 1½" high. Signed ©HAR on all pieces. $100.00 – 125.00.

HAR floral spray with matching clip earrings. The flowers are set with clear pavé rhinestones. The brooch is made in three pieces; the two flowers are riveted to the central piece. The pin measures 2½" x 2½"; the earrings measure 1" in diameter. Signed ©HAR on all pieces. $125.00 – 150.00.

109

Demi Parures and Parures

Maltese cross and fob style brooch is set in elegant gold-tone with matching clip earrings. An eagle sits atop a crown at the very top of the brooch which measures 3½" long. The brooch is signed FLORENZA© in a raised rectangle; the earrings are similarly signed and measure 1". $100.00 – 125.00.

This signed gold-tone brooch measures almost 3" long and has a large faux lapis cabochon as the focal point. The brooch features a crown design at the top, with smaller lapis cabochons and pearls as accents. Signed FLORENZA© in a raised rectangle. $50.00 – 75.00. The earrings coordinate nicely with the brooch, although they are not a match. They have pearls and clear rhinestones in a gold-tone setting with blue enamel and pearl centers. Measuring just over 1" in diameter, each is marked FLORENZA© stamped into the metal. $25.00 – 35.00.

Huge rhinestone pin and matching clip earrings set in shiny rhodium. I call this set the aurora borealis explosion. Unsigned. $75.00 – 100.00.

Demi Parures and Parures

Lovely and unusual demi parure has large pale blue rhinestones in the centers of the flowers. The earrings are clip back; only the brooch is marked WEISS without the copyright symbol. $125.00 – 150.00.

Pretty, dimensional floral pin features pale blue enameled petals with pearl cluster centers mounted on metal prongs. The brooch measures 3½" and is not marked. The matching clip back earrings are signed MARVELLA©. $50.00 – 75.00.

This brooch measures 2¼" in diameter and features a floral design with an outer ring of white opaque prong-set stones. Matching clip earrings measure 1" across. White glass jewelry is often referred to as milk glass. It reminds me of a time before season-less dressing when women wore pastel-colored clothing and white shoes beginning Memorial Day until Labor Day. Unsigned. $50.00 – 75.00.

111

Demi Parures and Parures

Another beautiful milk glass demi features a large brooch and matching clip earrings. All of the stones are prong-set and include white, pale green, and aurora borealis rhinestones. The brooch measures 2¾" long. The clip style earrings measure 1¾". $50.00 – 75.00.

Magnificent rhinestone brooch and matching earrings feature rich gold-tone leaf accents and pink, fuchsia, and pale lavender prong-set rhinestones. Each piece in this set features a central opaque pink speckled cabochon. Small aurora borealis stones encircle a central flower with a pretty pink rhinestone center. The earrings measure 1½"; the brooch is 2¾" x 2". The earrings are signed Carnegie. The brooch is signed Hattie Carnegie on an oval cartouche. $150.00 – 175.00.

I purchased this beautiful set many years ago. It is easily recognizable by collectors as being made by Hollycraft. What collectors appreciate about this jewelry, besides its excellent quality, is that Hollycraft founder Joseph Chorbajian both signed and dated Hollycraft jewelry. (Note: Some early Hollycraft jewelry was not marked.) The brooch features assorted sizes of rhinestones and measures 1¾" at its widest. It is signed HOLLYCRAFT on a raised rectangle; on another rectangle it is signed COPR.1950. The matching earrings are signed on the clip HOLLYCRAFT and again on a raised crescent HOLLYCRAFT COPR.1950. $75.00 – 100.00.

Demi Parures and Parures

Spectacular brooch with 12 large, luscious confetti rhinestones; each is surrounded by small aurora borealis rhinestones and all are prong-set in shiny rhodium. The brooch sits ¾" high and 2½" in diameter. Matching clip style earrings feature center confetti stones with dangling, prong-set aurora borealis rhinestones. These stunning earrings measure just over 2" long. Unsigned. $150.00 – 175.00.

High quality enameled brooch with orange and aurora borealis rhinestones in a floral design. This set is beautifully made with subtle accents; the rhinestones match the color of the enamel. The larger rhinestones are prong-set; the smaller are glued-in. The pin is signed on a rectangle SELINI©. The matching clip earrings are unsigned and measure 1½". Selini jewelry is high quality and hard to find; superior rhinestones and enameling in beautiful color combinations are hallmarks. $100.00 – 125.00.

This Sarah Coventry set named Fashion Splendor began to appear in their ads and catalogs beginning in 1961. The large pin features pink plastic and green rhinestones dotted with pearls in a circular gold-tone setting. The pin measures 2¾" in diameter and is marked ©SARAHCOV on a raised rectangle. The earrings are stamped ©SARAHCOV on the clips; they measure 1¼". $50.00 – 75.00.

113

Demi Parures and Parures

Lovely HAR brooch and matching clip earrings feature burnt orange center cabochons accented with tiny turquoise colored stones in an antiqued gold-tone setting. This set was also made with small green stones and matching bracelet (featured elsewhere in this book). The pin is very dimensional and measures 1" deep x 2" long. All pieces are similarly signed ©HAR on a raised rectangle. $100.00 – 125.00.

Fabulous wreath-shaped brooch has round and marquis-shaped cognac-colored rhinestones and an inner circle of chaton-cut aurora borealis rhinestones. The pin measures 2½" in diameter. The matching clip earrings measure 1½" long. All stones are prong-set. Unsigned. $50.00 – 75.00.

This lightweight, layered brooch features cognac-colored and plastic stones with an interesting mottled surface. All stones are prong-set. The pin is 3½" in length and a full 1" high. The matching clip earrings are as dimensional as the brooch, measure 1½" in length, and are very light weight. A lovely set, unsigned, however it may be the work of Beau Jewels. $125.00 – 150.00.

Demi Parures and Parures

This Sarah Coventry set was named Fashion Flower. The huge brooch measures 4" long x 1¾" across at its widest; it features red and aurora borealis rhinestones in a filigree gold-tone setting. It is shown with two pairs of matching earrings. One pair has flowers as huge as the brooch's floral centerpiece; the smaller earrings measure 1" across. The brooch is signed on the stem ©SARAHCOV. $75.00 – 100.00.

Kenneth Jay Lane earrings on original card are shown with matching ring. All are signed ©KENNETH LANE. The original purchase price was $5.00 for earrings and $5.00 for the ring. Price today $30.00 – 55.00 set. The inspiration for Mr. Lane's popular lion design comes from antique drawer pulls.

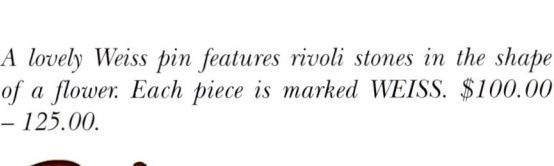

A lovely Weiss pin features rivoli stones in the shape of a flower. Each piece is marked WEISS. $100.00 – 125.00.

Demi Parures and Parures

Krementz petite circle pin with matching earrings is similar to one shown in the ad in Figure 22. Krementz jewelry is well made and very collectible. All pieces are signed KREMENTZ. $75.00 – 100.00 set.

Sarah Coventry chatelaine with matching clip earrings is from the early 1960s and was named Chit-Chat. With the chain removed the chatelaine converts to a pair of scatter pins. All pieces are marked ©SARAHCOV. $25.00 – 50.00.

Figure 22. Krementz vintage advertisement from LIFE magazine, December 4, 1964.

Demi Parures and Parures

Pretty petite Coro demi; all pieces are marked without the copyright symbol dating this piece to before the mid-1950s. (CORO was using the copyright symbol as early as 1947 so this set may have been even earlier.) Signed Coro. $50.00 – 75.00.

This Sarah Coventry set is named Touch of Elegance. Three gold-tone stems with prong-set green faceted fruit trimmed with gold-tone filigree caps are accented with green rhinestones. This is a lovely and elegant set aptly named. This set was made by DeLizza and Elster for Sarah Coventry. Signed ©SARAHCOV. $50.00 – 75.00.

Yellow and rose gold-tone chatelaine has prong-set blue glass stones. Each floral spray pin is marked STAR-ART 1/20 20 K G.F. Matching screw-back earrings are each marked 1/20 GOLDFILLED. $50.00 – 75.00.

117

Demi Parures and Parures

This is one of my favorite sets. The brooch in this lovely set is massive, measuring 4½" across. The brooch and clip back earrings feature faux pearls, aurora borealis rhinestones, and massive smoky topaz-colored stones. The set is surprisingly lightweight. It is unsigned except for a utility patent number (#2066969) on the pin's safety catch. The patent was issued on January 5, 1937, to Frank Farnham. Utility patents have seven-digit numbers and are issued for a practical and functional invention, in this case the safety clasp. Utility patents do not indicate the date of the jewelry since they could have been in use for 17 years or more. Unsigned. $150.00 – 200.00.

Huge swirling snowflake design brooch and matching earrings feature clear rhinestones in gold-tone settings. The brooch measures 4" in diameter. Unsigned. $50.00 – 75.00.

This surprisingly lightweight pin and matching clip earrings feature plastic textured stones which are glued in; the aurora borealis and citrine-colored stones are prong-set. The pin measures 2½" at its widest. Unsigned. $85.00 – 110.00.

118

Demi Parures and Parures

Luscious red rhinestone strawberry pin and earrings in japanned setting; note the green rhinestones in the stem. Marked WARNER on an oval cartouche. $150.00 – 175.00.

This graceful and dimensional set features enameled leaves interspersed with green rhinestones. The centers of the flowers are blue and green prong-set stones. The pin is signed VENDOME on an oval cartouche and the earrings are signed as well. $125.00 – 150.00.

Large retro style brooch has prong-set red stones and matching screw-back earrings. A 1940s brooch, it measures 4" x 4" and is marked STERLING. Each earring is marked STERLING on the screw back mechanism. $100.00 – 125.00.

Demi Parures and Parures

Large retro-style brooch with calla lilies is set in rose gold-tone; matching pale rose colored pearls are the flower centers. The brooch measures over 4" long and is accompanied by matching screw-back earrings. Unsigned. $50.00 – 75.00.

The petite demi has tiny pearls covering the surface. The pin and earrings are accented with small opaque cabochons in blue, green, and red. Unsigned. $50.00 – 75.00.

Enameled copper brooch is in the shape of an artist's palette. The earrings are matching, smaller palettes each accented with two paint brushes. The pin is marked Matisse in script on the pin clasp; both earrings are marked Matisse on earring backs. This is a classic and collectible set, easy for collectors to identify. $100.00 – 125.00.

Demi Parures and Parures

Sarah Coventry set named Bittersweet dates from August 1962 and perhaps earlier. Gold-tone leaves with coral tear-drop inserts and matching clip earrings make this an attractive set. The brooch is large and measures 3½" long. $50.00 – 75.00.

Orange, yellow, and green enameled flower has matching earrings, accented by clear and orange rhinestones. The glass center stones in both the pin and earrings have a marbled effect. The brooch measures 2½" in diameter. Unsigned. $35.00 – 60.00.

Petite ballerina measures just 1½" tall and has green, brown, and orange thermoplastic insets in a gold-tone setting; the earrings are not an exact match but coordinate nicely with the pin. Unsigned. $20.00 – 35.00 for pin and earrings.

121

Demi Parures and Parures

Unsigned demi in the colors of fall features open-back unfoiled, prong-set rhinestones; matching earrings have dangling stones. The brooch is a spray of flowers, one deep red with golden topaz center, the other a lighter topaz with deeper golden center. All stones are prong-set; even the brooch stem is studded with prong-set rhinestones. Unsigned, probably DeLizza and Elster. $100.00 – 125.00.

A striking brooch with matching earrings feature opaque stones in a japanned setting. The center of the flower is a cluster of orange rhinestones. Unsigned. $50.00 – 75.00.

Jet black rhinestones are featured in a japanned setting; a patent pending number is the only mark on the back of the clip earrings. This set reminds me of the early 1960s jewelry produced by Albert Weiss. Unsigned. $35.00 – 60.00.

122

Demi Parures and Parures

Mandolin brooch with matching earrings; the almost-olive green enamel is accented with iridescent green and pink stripes in a Mod design. This interesting set is signed KARU Arké INC. $35.00 – 60.00.

This Sarah Coventry set is named Cameo Lace. Powder blue plastic cameos are set in a lattice design gold-tone setting. The set is marked SC in an oval cartouche. $25.00 – 40.00.

Leaf design brooch and matching clip earrings feature a glittery, molded plastic background trimmed with yellow and clear rhinestones. Only the earrings are marked Coro in script. $50.00 – 75.00.

Demi Parures and Parures

Large Sarah Coventry brooch named Radiance features large clear rhinestones in a gold-tone setting with matching clip earrings. Signed ©SARAHCOV. $50.00 – 75.00.

This beautiful set features large pearl centers in both the brooch and earrings. The earrings are signed JUDY LEE in capital letters; the brooch is similarly signed on a raised rectangle. The Judy Lee Company marketed jewelry much like Sarah Coventry, Emmons, and Tara through in-home shows. The popularity of Judy Lee jewelry is growing in the collectibles market. $50.00 – 75.00.

This Sarah Coventry brooch with matching earrings features large center pearls in silver-tone settings. The brooch was shown in a 1963 Cosmopolitan magazine ad being worn in the model's hair and on a sheath-style dress strap. Signed SARAHCOV©. $50.00 – 75.00.

Demi Parures and Parures

Sarah Coventry silver-tone strawberry pin and matching earrings were named Strawberry Ice. The pin is marked ©SARAHCOV; the matching earrings are faintly marked on the earring clips SARAH COV and PAT PEND. The pin is just over 2" long x 1½" wide. $25.00 – 50.00.

Another favorite among Sarah Coventry collectors, this set was named Bird of Paradise and features aurora borealis rhinestones in a graceful silver-tone setting. The matching earrings are clip-style. $50.00 – 75.00.

Very nice quality diamante butterfly in rhodium setting has matching clip-style earrings. Unsigned. $25.00 – 50.00.

Demi Parures and Parures

Petite silver wreath has matching earrings. The pin is signed KREMENTZ on the pin mechanism; the screw-back earrings are also signed KREMENTZ on the curved post. Krementz jewelry features classic and elegant designs. It was made using high quality materials and features excellent workmanship. $75.00 – 100.00.

Brooch and matching earrings have crystals and rhinestone encrusted dangling balls. Amazingly, all of the rhinestones are prong-set! Unsigned. $50.00 – 75.00.

A bit of nostalgia from Atlantic City, this wood circle pin and matching clip earrings were purchased as a souvenir on the boardwalk in 1960. Unsigned. $20.00 – 35.00.

Demi Parures and Parures

Avon tribal mask with matching pierced earrings is an especially well made set with colorful rhinestone accents and lots of detail. The large pin measures 3" from top to bottom. All pieces are similarly signed ©AVON. $50.00 – 75.00.

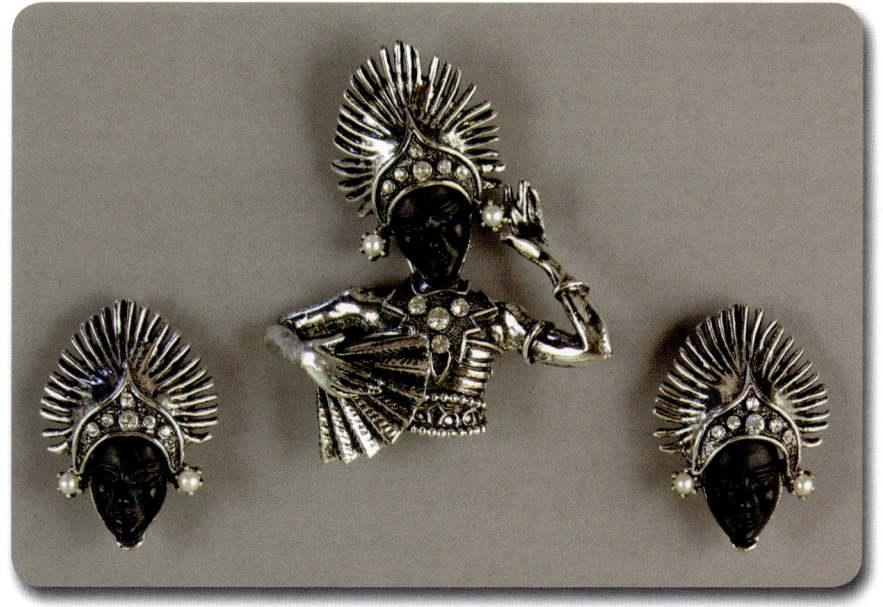

Matching brooch and earrings feature dancing Blackamoor princess with black thermoplastic face, elaborate headdress, faux pearl earrings, and clear rhinestones in a silver-tone setting. The earrings are unsigned; the pin is marked PAM©. PAM jewelry is considered by collectors to be of average quality. Still, the design of this set is very striking. The value is increased because it is a matched set in excellent condition. $150.00 – 175.00.

Fabulous Asian princess brooch has a green plastic face and elaborate, pearl-encrusted headdress decorated with rows of clear rhinestones. The brooch measures 3¾" tall. The clip earrings feature a less ornate headdress and measure 1½". The quality of these stunning pieces definitely suggests designer-made. Unsigned. Brooch, $125.00 – 150.00. Earrings, $35.00 – 60.00.

127

Demi Parures and Parures

Top center: Scarf clip marked PAT. PEND. probably for the scarf clip mechanism. This piece features aurora borealis and lava stone trim but is unsigned. $100.00 – 125.00. Bottom: The bottom center gold-tone brooch is almost 2½" tall and features a plastic, ivory-colored face with hat, trimmed with aurora borealis rhinestones, two green cabochons, and one small lava stone (lower left). The matching earrings flank the brooch; only one earring and the brooch are signed ©HAR. $200.00 – 250.00. The figures without hats are clip earrings and measure 1¼" high. Only one earring is marked ©HAR. $100.00 – 125.00.

Top: Smiling Asian figural pendant is made like the brooch on the left and is signed ART©. Left: This brooch features three green cabochons with aurora borealis trim in shiny gold-tone setting and measures 2½" tall. Signed ART©. Bottom: The clip earrings may be on their original store card; this is how I purchased them. Both are marked ©ART and, like the brooch, are strikingly similar to HAR Asian figural jewelry. Right: The adjustable ring is an unusual piece and is signed ART©. It features aurora borealis rhinestones and center green cabochon. $325.00 – 375.00 all pieces.

Asian figural pendant is similar in body style to the HAR and ART figures, but without the rhinestone trim. Another difference is that the face is ceramic. Just the pendant measures 3" and is shown with a gold-tone box chain. The pendant is signed NAPIER© and so is the chain. A similar figure was made by Napier to be worn as a brooch. $100.00 – 125.00.

Demi Parures and Parures

Brightly colored orange enameled Buddha pendant is set in elaborate gold-tone. Every link on the accompanying gold-tone chain features a design. The coordinating enamel clip-back earrings and pendant are signed ART© on a raised rectangle. $100.00 – 125.00.

Antiqued and textured gold-tone setting with a rope-like design are featured in this bracelet, earrings, and brooch. Green stones with large, burnt orange center cabochons in the pin and earrings add to the lovely design. Pin and earrings are signed HAR©; the bracelet is not signed. $275.00 – 325.00.

Pretty parure with earrings, bracelet, and necklace features Buddha-style plastic figures and emerald green rhinestones; note the dragon motif on the necklace and bracelet. The necklace measures 16½" and the length can be adjusted; bracelet measures 7¾"; and the clip earrings measure 1¼". Unsigned. $150.00 – 200.00.

Demi Parures and Parures

Interesting and well made parure features detailed Asian figures in gold-tone settings. The set includes pendant, bracelet, and matching clip earrings. The figures in the necklace and bracelet match. The large pendant measures 3" high x 2¼" wide; the earrings measure 1¼" high. The figures have the appearance of aged ivory. The bracelet and one earring are signed COLCO©. The pendant is not signed. Colco jewelry is rare in the collectibles market and sometimes not signed. As a result, it can be mistakenly attributed to HAR, Selro, Selini, or even Hobé. $175.00 – 225.00.

HAR genie parure, top: Genie clip earrings feature detailed figures with fancy turbans that match other pieces in this series. $250.00 – 300.00. Left: Standing genie brooch presents his crystal ball on a tray. His skin has a coppery finish; his harem pants and vest are a pretty gold-tone. This figural measures 2½" high and is signed ©HAR. $500.00 – 600.00. Center genie: There is so much detail in this piece. The genie wears a richly detailed vest with clear rhinestone trim. He is also wearing arm bands and even the base of the Lucite crystal ball is trimmed with rhinestones. The brooch measures 2¼" high. Signed ©HAR. $500.00 – 600.00. Right: HAR mermaid with crystal ball that features a golden fish. Her headdress is accented by a red rhinestone in the center of the forehead. This expressive piece measures 2" x 2". Signed ©HAR. $500.00 – 600.00. Bottom: Matching genie bracelet is simply stunning and features many details including links with a magic lantern, ornate palace, and genie with crystal ball. The genie's turban is decorated with a ruby red cabochon. The final link also has a large cabochon. Clear rhinestones provide additional accents. A safety chain is included for good measure. The bracelet is not signed. $800.00 – 1,000.00.

Demi Parures and Parures

HAR dragon parure includes necklace, clamper bracelet, earrings, and brooch. Without a doubt, these stunning pieces are among the finest and most beautiful costume jewelry ever made. The necklace features beautifully rendered green enamel links shaped like reptilian scales. The rhinestones are mostly large and iridescent in irregular shapes. Signed HAR©. $3,500.00 – 3,800.00.

It's easy to run out of adjectives when describing the HAR fantasy pieces. The rare and exquisite HAR cobra necklace is made with green enameling and colored glass stones. This piece is signed HAR©. $2,000.00 – 2,500.00.

Bright turquoise thermoplastic Asian princess in a bolo-style necklace has matching wide bracelet and clip earrings. These sets are sought after by collectors. Unsigned. $175.00 – 225.00.

Demi Parures and Parures

Dangling pendant necklace and matching clip earrings are mounted in silver-tone settings with red enameled and thermoplastic accents. The style is suggestive of the work of Selro. Very often, Selro pieces were unmarked except for a hang tag on the jewelry which was removed before wearing. Unsigned. $125.00 – 150.00.

Stunning faux turquoise and coral cabochons make up this necklace and bracelet demi. The bracelet is shown open to reveal that the entire surface is encrusted with plastic cabochons to match the spectacular Asian inspired necklace. The pendant measures over 4" long including the dangling beads. Each piece is signed Hobé on an oval cartouche. $150.00 – 175.00.

Beautiful turquoise blue enamel on copper. The necklace measures 17" long; the bracelet measures 7½". The matching earrings are screwback. The bracelet and necklace are signed Matisse; the earrings are unsigned. $225.00 – 275.00.

Demi Parures and Parures

Avon set from the Duchess Collection by Kenneth Jay Lane includes panther bracelet, necklace, and matching clip earrings. The exotic set features a 19" choker of single strand, shiny pearl gray beads. The earrings measure 1" and feature emerald green colored stones. The clamper-style bangle is similar in design to the earrings. All pieces are signed K.J.L. for AVON on an oval cartouche. $125.00 – 175.00.

Etruscan-look necklace from the 1980s features peach plastic cabochons and dangling seed pearls in a matte gold-tone finish. The center medallion is encircled with tiny pearls for a delicate and beautiful touch. The small black cabochons provide a striking contrast. The gold-tone earrings have the same rich matte finish and coordinate nicely with the necklace but are not an exact match. All pieces are similarly signed CRAFT© on an oval cartouche. $50.00 – 75.00 for the necklace; $20.00 – 35.00 for the earrings.

Large oval hematite pendant with matching earrings are featured in a heavy and ornate silver-tone setting. The pendant measures 2½" long x 2" wide on an 18" chain. The pendant is marked Whiting & Davis Co Bags; the earrings are marked only Whiting & Davis on the clip mechanism. $50.00 – 75.00.

Demi Parures and Parures

This lovely parure is made up of black diamonds and clear baguettes in a rhodium setting. The pretty X design is accented with clear baguettes. The necklace also features marquis-shaped stones throughout. The bracelet is 7½" long; the necklace measures 15" long, and the earrings measure 1". All pieces in this lovely set are marked KRAMER©. $125.00 – 175.00.

A magnificent full parure from the Trifari Wildflower collection includes necklace, bracelet, brooch, and matching clip earrings; all pieces but the earrings have their original tags. Plastic flower clusters feature gold centers and clear rhinestone accents in a matte gold-tone setting. There are 14 flower clusters in the necklace alone. All pieces are similarly stamped with the crown TRIFARI© symbol. $250.00 – 300.00.

Beautiful Egyptian revival parure by Eugene is strikingly similar to a collar and matching earrings by Miriam Haskell circa 1955 (as seen in Amazing Gems by Deanna Farnetti Cera). What adds to the value of this lovely set is its rarity; it is the only full parure by Eugene that I have ever seen. Egyptian revival jewelry is extremely popular and sought after by collectors. Signed Eugene. $800.00 – 1,000.00.

When he began making jewelry for his company in 1952, Eugene opened a showroom on Madison Avenue in New York City. His jewelry was also sold at upscale department stores including Saks Fifth Avenue and Neiman Marcus. All of his jewelry was made by hand. He was only in business for about 10 years.

Demi Parures and Parures

Pale blue rhinestone set includes bracelet, necklace, screw back earrings, and cascading style brooch. Every single rhinestone in this lovely set is prong-set. Unsigned. $125.00 – 150.00.

Unusual Sceptron parure features brooch, bracelet, and matching screw-back earrings. The earrings are unsigned; the brooch is signed SCEPTRON STERLING which is imprinted in the metal. The bracelet is marked 12K/20GF. This fabulous Art Deco design set is accented with clear and blue stones which are all prong-set. 275.00 – 325.00.

Patriotic necklace, earrings, bracelet, and flag brooch features red, white, and blue rhinestones in a shiny gold-tone setting. Every rhinestone in every piece is prong-set. Unsigned. $50.00 – 75.00.

Demi Parures and Parures

Hobé marketed a line of gorgeous and ornate rhinestone jewelry which was called Jewels of Legendary Splendor. When collectors come across a set like this, it is easy to understand how the marketing folks came up with the name. I purchased this lovely full parure in its original box. Every single stone in this fabulous parure is prong-set. The bracelet features clear sparkling center baguettes accented by rows of square aurora borealis rhinestones. The bracelet measures 7" long x 2" wide. The bracelet is signed Hobé on the back of the clasp. The necklace features a row of clear baguettes and aurora borealis rhinestones above a grid of pearls and crystals. Even the adjustable clasp is decorated with a dangling crystal. The matching earrings are clip style. One earring is marked Hobé on the clip mechanism; the other is marked PAT. PEND. The earrings have small plastic cylinders on the top of the clips for comfort. $350.00 – 400.00.

It is hard to describe (and even harder to capture) the beauty of this Mazer demi. Both feature large emerald-cut aurora borealis rhinestones with clear chaton and baguette rhinestone accents. The bracelet measures 7½" long and has a safety chain. The necklace measures 15" long. The bracelet is marked Joseph Mazer. The necklace is marked MAZER. Simply stunning. $450.00 – 500.00.

This Sarah Coventry necklace with matching earrings is named Golden Avocado. The pendant can be worn as shown on the center, horizontal chain. Or that chain can be removed and worn as a bracelet, while the pendant slides onto the longer, 30" chain for a different look. Only the earrings are signed SARAHCOV©. $35.00 – 50.00. Sarah Coventry jewelry was made to be versatile. One of the features of home parties was that a Sarah Coventry representative and/or hostess could demonstrate the many ways their jewelry could be worn to accent an outfit. In one 1973 promotional ad for Sarah Coventry chains, women were encouraged to "wear three or more all at once…wrap one around your wrist as a bracelet."

Demi Parures and Parures

Crystal and bead necklace and earrings are shown with original hard plastic box. The necklace and earrings originally sold for $2.00 each. Now just the boxes can sell on eBay for $20.00 and above. The set is in excellent condition, with original tags, and is part of the Crown Jewels Collection made by Laguna. The tag on the necklace is marked Crown Jewel Look as is the inside of the box. The clasp on the necklace is marked LAGUNA. Laguna Crown Jewels are featured in a snazzy vintage ad shown in Figure 23. $125.00 – 150.00 for all pieces including the jewelry box.

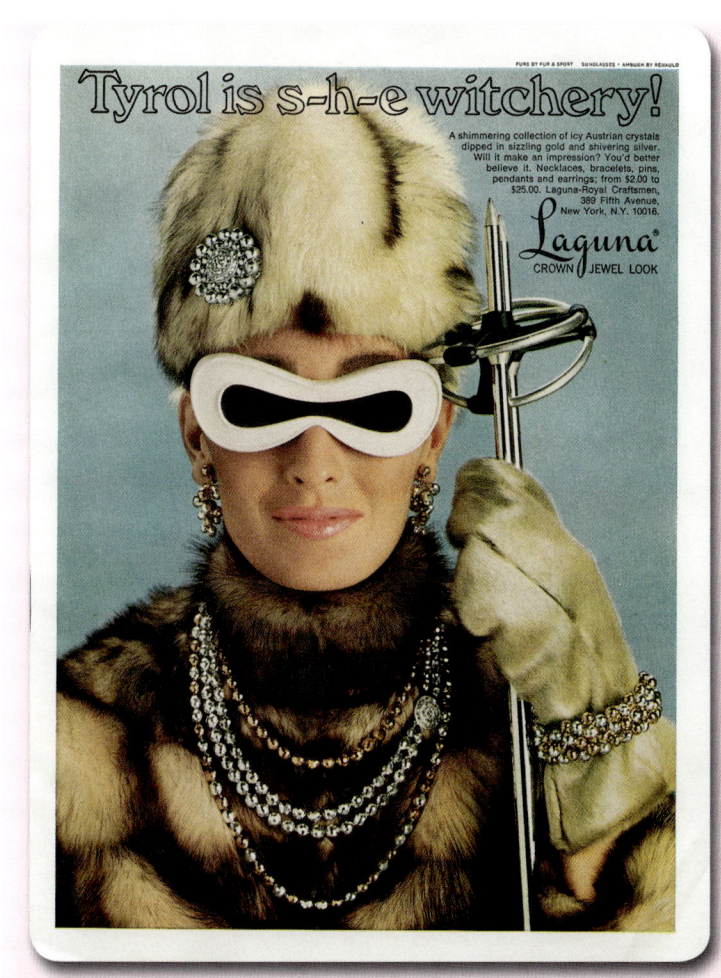

Figure 23. Laguna vintage advertisement from *Harper's Bazaar* magazine.

Lovely demi features a fancy filigree gold-tone setting with pearls, lavender and purple prong-set rhinestones, and a large center cabochon. Note the gold-tone heart and other pretty details on the chain near the pendant. The matching earrings are stamped WGERMANY on the clips. $65.00 – 90.00.

137

Demi Parures and Parures

Double strand iridescent crystal necklace with tiny crystal spacers and a beautiful square centerpiece is accented with pearls and aurora borealis rhinestones. The matching clip earrings are stamped WEISS on the back of the clip mechanism. $75.00 – 100.00.

This adjustable necklace has plastic blue flowers with rhinestone centers in a silver-tone setting. Only the matching earrings are marked Coro in script. $35.00 – 60.00.

Pastel-colored pink, blue, and yellow plastic flowers with rhinestone centers make this necklace and matching screw-back earrings a perfect spring/summer look. The necklace is marked Coro without the copyright symbol; the earrings are marked Coro on the earring screw-back mechanisms. The necklace is adjustable and is marked PAT PEND with other illegible letters or numbers near the Coro signature on the back. This necklace is very similar to patent 172349 issued to A. Katz on June 1, 1954, shown in Figure 24. $50.00 – 75.00.

Demi Parures and Parures

This triple strand, choker style beaded necklace features textured silver and gold beads, matte gold-tone beads, and pretty iridescent glass beads. It is stamped HONG KONG on the clasp. The earring beads are strung with wire and attached to a metal back. They are marked on the clip mechanism HONG KONG. $35.00 – 50.00.

Figure 24. Copy of A. Katz patent for necklace or the like.

Pretty pavé-set diamante heart pendant on silver-tone chain has a fold-over clasp. The heart measures 1" x 1". The matching earrings are screw-back and measure ¾" x ¾". A feminine set, unsigned. $35.00 – 50.00.

Demi Parures and Parures

Plastic floral necklace has golden topaz and citrine-colored rhinestones. Some of the flowers are encircled with pearls. Matching clip earrings complete the ensemble. The necklace and one clip earring in this lovely demi are signed ART© on a raised rectangle. $50.00 – 75.00.

Enameled demi features pretty pastel colors of lavender, aqua, and cream. The flower brooch measures a full 3" long. The earrings are not marked; both the flower and bangle are marked KRAMER© on a raised rectangle. The unsigned genie brooch is made is two pieces. $75.00 – 100.00.

This necklace has a triple strand of iridescent turquoise colored crystals and alternating beads with gold wash. The earrings are hand wired and signed VOGUE. $75.00 – 100.00.

Necklaces

Lovely high quality triple strand necklace has opaque blue beads and crystals. It is accented with twisted glass beads and ornate gold-tone caps on the beads. The set has matching clip-back earrings that are adjustable. The necklace is marked on the clasp VENDOME©. $100.00 – 125.00.

Necklaces

This striking Nettie Rosenstein necklace features large pink cameos encircled with clear rhinestones mounted on a triple chain. The center cameo is marked STERLING and Nettie Rosenstein in script on a raised rectangle. Like Hattie Carnegie, Coco Chanel, and Elsa Schiaparelli, Ms. Rosenstein was a clothing designer who made jewelry to coordinate with her fashions. Her jewelry is rare and very collectible. $175.00 – 200.00.

Stunning Schiaparelli necklace has three large flowers with petals of molten faux pearls, black diamonds, and aurora borealis centers; the necklace also has beautiful opaque cognac-colored rhinestones all in a shiny rhodium setting. The necklace is signed is two places Schiaparelli. Every stone is prong-set in this take-your-breath-away later example of Schiaparelli genius. $400.00 – 500.00.

Necklaces

Spectacular Egyptian motif pendant on heavy gold-tone chain. The pendant measures just over 3½" long x 2½" at its widest. The focal point is a large, faux jade stone held in place by four substantial prongs. The colorful accents are enameled. The piece is marked CASTLECLIFF on a raised rectangle. $150.00 – 175.00.

Substantial gold-tone necklace has green cabochons set in heavy gold-tone discs. This necklace has a T-bar clasp and weighs almost 9 ounces! It is signed GIVENCHY PARIS on an oval cartouche. $175.00 – 200.00.

Very detailed Egyptian Revival style necklace in an antiqued gold-tone setting has three dangling chains, each accented with a charm. The chain features a fold-over clasp and is stamped ©ART on the back. $50.00 – 75.00.

142

Necklaces

Oriental dragon pendant in shiny gold-tone with dangles is accented with coral-colored plastic rods and beads. The chain features a fold-over clasp. The pendant is signed ©ART in two places including on the back of the dragon and at the top back of the pendant. $50.00 – 75.00.

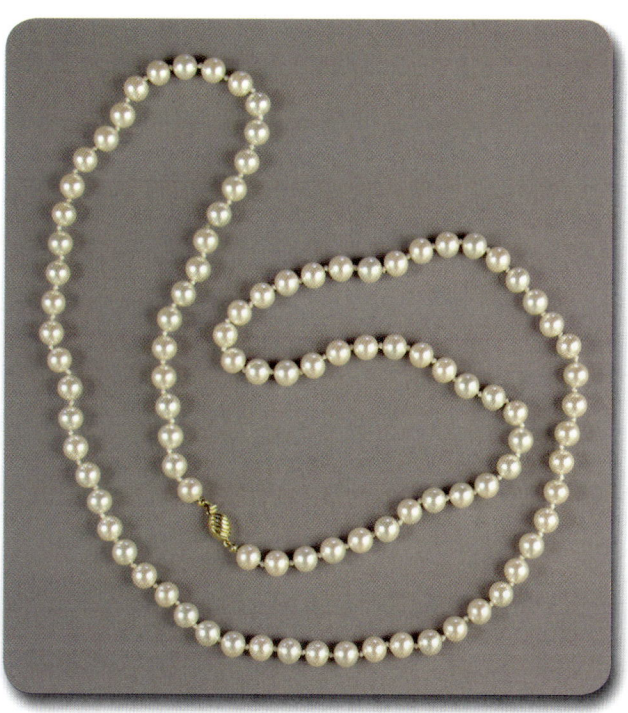

A fabulous 30" strand of faux pearls signed MARVELLA® on the metal clasp — to twist, to twine, to drape! $35.00 – 50.00.

Very well made and richly enameled frog is mounted on a heavy gold chain. Signed LES BERNARD INC. $40.00 – 65.00.

143

Necklaces

Hobé gold-tone and coral plastic necklace depicts a sage with beard and tablet. The figure measures almost 2" tall and is very detailed. The attached chain has an Asian symbol where the pendant is attached. Signed Hobé on the bottom of the figure. 75.00 – 100.00.

Left: Gorgeous green and gold-tone cameo locket has an elaborate setting. The locket is marked on the inside FLORENZA© on a raised rectangle. The chain is 30" long and has no clasp. $50.00 – 75.00. Right: A gold-tone pendant on 30" chain is marked with the crown TRIFARI© signature. $35.00 – 60.00.

Fabulous necklace has six strands of beads including pearls and blue and red glass beads between matte gold-tone beads. The necklace measures 16½" in length including clasp. Unsigned. $100.00 – 125.00.

144

Necklaces

Top: Adjustable choker necklace has aurora borealis rhinestones in a fancy setting; clear rhinestones provide accents. Signed Coro on the clasp. $25.00 – 50.00. Second down: Shiny gold-tone adjustable necklace has gold leaves and clusters of aurora borealis rhinestones. A very well made, heavy piece which is signed LISNER on the hook. $50.00 – 75.00. Third down: Adjustable choker necklace features iridescent striated emerald green stones accented with small matching green rhinestones. A very pretty effect, signed Coro. $25.00 – 50.00. Bottom: Beautiful translucent leaf shaped plastic inserts are accented with aurora borealis rhinestones in this stunning silver-tone necklace with adjustable clasp. Signed LISNER on top of clasp hook. $50.00 – 75.00.

A purple intaglio disk is the centerpiece of this pretty necklace featuring a 28" chain. The triple strands are accented with purple discs. Stamped GOLDETTE© on the metal clasp. $50.00 – 75.00.

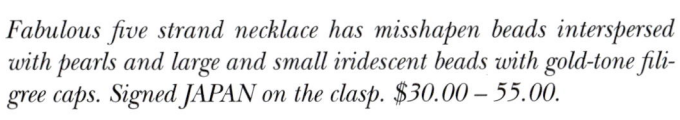

Fabulous five strand necklace has misshapen beads interspersed with pearls and large and small iridescent beads with gold-tone filigree caps. Signed JAPAN on the clasp. $30.00 – 55.00.

145

Necklaces

Ornate cross in antiqued gold setting has clear, prong-set rhinestone accents. The bail is marked with the Lion passant and the letters CAL; the Lion passant signifies the piece is British sterling silver. If the piece is made in the U.S. the word STERLING usually appears also. I added the chain. $75.00 – 100.00.

Pretty triple strand choker necklace features a center gold-tone rose accented by a pearl and fold over clasp. Unsigned. $50.00 – 75.00.

Topaz-colored rhinestone necklace has variegated ivory-colored plastic inserts. All of the stones are prong-set. Unsigned. $25.00 – 50.00.

Bracelets

Lovely Victorian revival bracelet features green plastic inserts and pearl accents with a wide fold over clasp. The bracelet measures 1½" x 7½". The matching clip earrings feature the same green plastic inserts with pearl accents. This set resembles Florenza and Tara jewelry but is unsigned. $35.00 – 60.00.

Top: Delicate, antiqued gold-tone faux slide bracelet has charms that do not move along a chain as they would on a true slide bracelet. Signed ©ART. $35.00 – 60.00. *Middle:* This bracelet is a true slide bracelet. It has lots of detail including pearls, many colored stones, a plastic cameo, and a fly, in an antiqued gold-tone setting. It is unmarked but similar in style to jewelry made by Goldette. $35.00 – 60.00. *Bottom:* This shiny gold-tone bracelet is also a true slide bracelet. It features unusual stones including a speckled Easter egg, faux turquoise, plastic prong-set cameo, and carved faux jade stone. Unsigned. $100.00 – 125.00.

Top: Bright aqua and cocoa colored thermoplastic bracelet in a silver-tone setting. Unsigned. $25.00 – 40.00. *Middle:* Aqua colored thermoplastic bracelet in a shiny silver-tone setting. The bracelet measures 7½". Unsigned. $25.00 – 40.00. *Bottom:* Unusual petal-shaped plastic inserts are in a matte finish silver-tone setting with wide fold-over clasp. Unsigned. $25.00 – 40.00.

147

Bracelets

Top: The photograph does not do justice to this feminine and graceful gold-tone filigree bracelet with aurora borealis stones throughout. Unsigned. $40.00 – 65.00. Middle: Confetti Lucite cabochons with pearl accents are featured in this wide (1½") gold-tone bracelet. Unsigned. $35.00 – 60.00. Bottom: DeLizza and Elster (Juliana) style five-link design in antiqued gold-tone has turquoise and gold flecked center stones accented with pretty pale blue rhinestones. Wide fold-over clasp, unsigned. $100.00 – 125.00.

Variations on a theme. Asian faces in ivory-colored thermoplastic are trimmed with faux pearls and set in gold-tone. Unsigned. $75.00 – 100.00. Asian faces in black thermoplastic are trimmed with faux pearls and red rhinestones and set in silver-tone. Unsigned. $75.00 – 100.00.

Ornate, antiqued gold-tone bracelet features whimsical ivory-colored thermoplastic faces. The bracelet has a wide fold-over clasp, is accented with green cabochons and lavender rhinestones, and measures 7½" long. SELRO jewelry like this has become very collectible and is getting harder to find. Stamped SELRO CORP.©. $175.00 – 200.00.

Bracelets

Left to right: Opulent and ornate antiqued gold-tone bangle has pin clasp and safety chain. Large and small faux prong-set turquoise and seed pearls accent this bangle bracelet, given to me by my aunt. Unsigned. $150.00 – 175.00. Victorian revival bracelet with tiny pearl and faux turquoise and amethyst accents. Unsigned. $35.00 – 60.00. Opulent antiqued gold-tone bangle with pearl and faux amethyst accents. Unsigned. $150.00 – 175.00. Early 1900s gold-tone filigree setting has amethyst colored stones. Unsigned. $75.00 – 100.00. Rich antiqued gold-tone bangle has multicolored stones. Unsigned. $150.00 – 175.00. Beautiful early Victorian revival slide bracelet/bangle with pearls and blue enamel. Unsigned. $100.00 – 125.00.

Left to Right: Damascene style wide (1½") bracelet has double v-spring box clasp and safety chain. The bracelet's panels are prong-set. Unsigned. $35.00 – 60.00. Unique locket bracelet has five links but only three open. One features a picture of a little boy with a baseball bat slung over his shoulder. Signed twice Hattie Carnegie on an oval cartouche with a nearby ©. $100.00 – 125.00. Gold-tone curlicues are featured in this 17 link bracelet with fold-over clasp and safety chain. It is signed MONET© on a hang tag. $35.00 – 60.00. Copper link bracelet with highly stylized leaf design. The bracelet is 1¾" wide and signed Rebajes. $100.00 – 125.00. Heavy and wide (1¾") four-link gold-tone bracelet has window pane design accented with gold balls. Signed CADORO© on an oval cartouche. $75.00 – 100.00.

Bracelets

Top: Repeating leaf design features aurora borealis rhinestones in shiny rhodium. Bracelet measures ¾" wide x 7½". Signed Coro© on clasp. $35.00 – 60.00. Middle: Reticulated panther design bracelet is set with clear rhinestones. The Duchess of Windsor's cat jewelry was probably the inspiration for this and many other similarly designed bracelets. Unsigned. $50.00 – 75.00. Bottom: Double X design bracelet is accented with chaton-cut rhinestones. It has a wide, fold-over clasp which is signed with the Pegasus symbol and Coro©. $35.00 – 60.00.

Left to right: Two rows of prong-set rhinestones are accented with pear-shaped stones in the center of the bracelet. Signed GARNE JEWELRY on the clasp. $40.00 – 65.00. Three rows of tiny, prong-set rhinestones are accented with rectangular-shaped rhinestones in the center of the middle row. Unsigned. $25.00 – 50.00. Elegant Art Deco design bracelet is signed MAZER and the number 27. $40.00 – 65.00. This bracelet features two rows of diamante rhinestones. Unsigned. $50.00 – 75.00. Domed bracelet measures ¾" wide. Every stone is prong-set. Signed WEISS. $75.00 – 100.00. Tiny prong-set rhinestones are accented with center navettes and round stones. Unsigned. $25.00 – 50.00. Stretch bracelets were popular in the 1950s. This one features over 90 prong-set clear rhinestones. Marked MADE IN BRITISH HONG KONG and BRAND NEW YORK. $40.00 – 65.00.

Magnificent rhinestone bracelet by Kramer. The citrine, topaz, and green rhinestones are set in gold-tone and feature icing, the small curls set with rhinestones that were more commonly found on Eisenberg and some Weiss rhinestone jewelry. Signed KRAMER of N.Y. on the clasp. $100.00 – 125.00.

Bracelets

Top: Christmas charms are featured on this wide link bracelet. The charms include holly, stars, bells, and a Christmas tree. Unsigned. $30.00 – 55.00. Middle: Antiqued gold-tone bracelet with filigree charms including a large center one, and carved Bakelite balls. The bracelet is marked but I cannot make out the signature. $50.00 – 75.00. Bottom: The size of the charms belie the weight of this bracelet. It is actually very lightweight and features big chunks of plastic, gold leaves, and small plastic balls. Some of the big pieces of plastic are wrapped with gold-tone wire. A fun bracelet. Unsigned. $25.00 – 50.00.

Very collectible and beautiful Weiss plastic clamper bracelet studded with clear and pastel rhinestones. The earrings are not marked; the bracelet is marked WEISS on the gold-tone hinge. $175.00 – 225.00.

Heavy bangle bracelet with bands of glittery copper and brown, accented with two rows of channel-set rhinestones. The bracelet measures 2" wide and is signed LES BERNARD INC on an oval cartouche. $35.00 – 60.00.

151

Bracelets

Gold-tone cuff-style bracelet features raised flowers with red prong-set rhinestones. It also features a diagonal row of small red rhinestones. Signed KENNETH LANE©. $50.00 – 75.00.

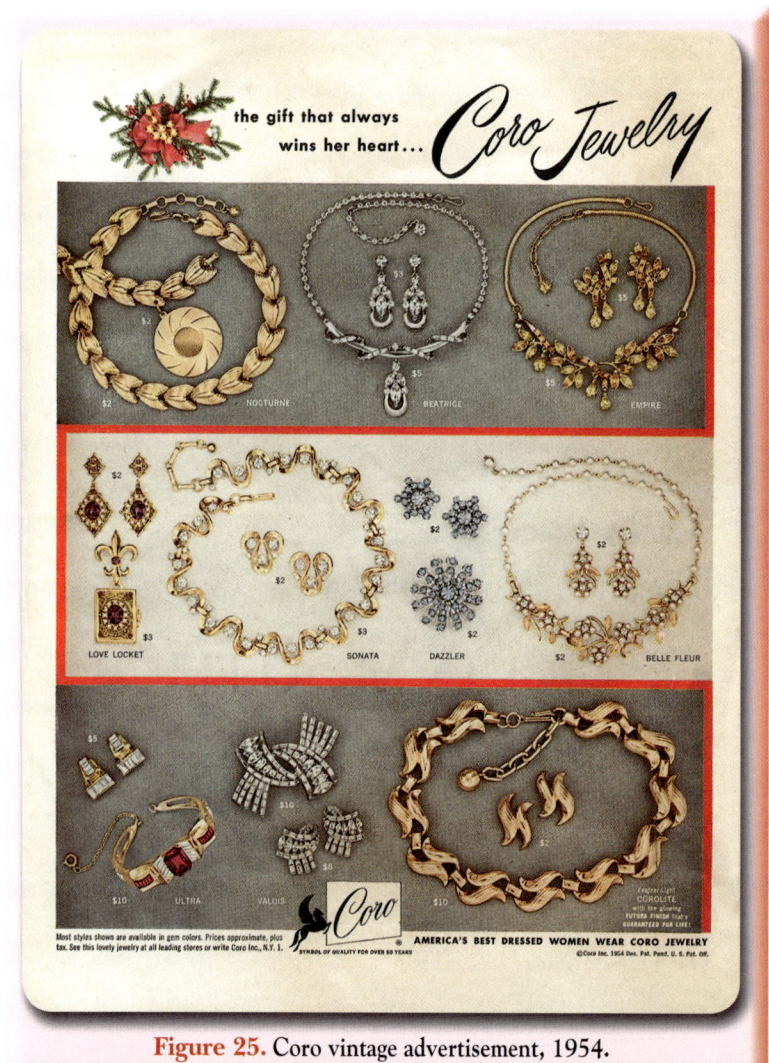

Figure 25. Coro vintage advertisement, 1954.

Gold-tone bangle bracelet with safety chain is set with red and clear baguettes on either side of the large emerald-cut center stone. I was fortunate to find the original ad which helps to date this piece to 1954 (see Figure 25). Signed Corocraft DES.PAT.PEND on a raised rectangle. $75.00 – 100.00.

Earrings

Similarly designed earrings in different sizes. Top: This pair features pearl centers with channel-set clear rhinestones. Unsigned. $15.00 – 25.00. Bottom: This set has white plastic cabochons surrounded by channel-set rhinestones. Unsigned. $20.00 – 35.00.

Top: Pretty dangling earrings are signed NEWHOUSE and feature delicate gold-tone chains. $20.00 – 30.00. Center: Small, high quality pearls in the center measure just ¾" wide and are marked MIMI d N © 1978 on a raised rectangle. Both earrings are marked. Mimi di Niscemi began producing jewelry in the early 1960s until late 1970. She set up her own company in 1962 in New York and her creations became popular very quickly. $25.00 – 35.00. Bottom: The fan-shaped gold-tone earrings are set with a large pearl and pavé rhinestones; they are marked PARKLANE on an oval cartouche. $15.00 – 25.00.

Top: Pretty yellow enameled flower earrings marked TRIFARI. $20.00 – 30.00. Bottom: Clear Lucite wave-shaped earrings are topped with shimmering yellow plastic are set with various sizes of yellow and aurora borealis rhinestones. Clip style, unsigned. $20.00 – 30.00.

153

Earrings

Top: DeLizza & Elster style earrings with open backs and unusual stones. Unsigned. $35.00 – 50.00. Bottom: Beautifully made domed clip earrings are accented with center pearls which are encircled with fuchsia rhinestones and faux turquoise. They measure 1" in diameter and are signed HAR©. $25.00 – 40.00.

Top: Pearl and orange rhinestone clip earrings signed HAR©. $25.00 – 40.00. Bottom: Rectangular clip earrings are unsigned except for a utility patent number. A variety of beautiful stones are found in these earrings including pearls, faux turquoise, coral, and colorful rhinestones, all prong-set. $25.00 – 40.00.

Top: Pink enameled clip style earrings have gold-tone centers and are signed PASTELLI. Little is known about this company except that they produced pastel-colored jewelry. I have only seen pieces without rhinestones, although they also produced rhinestone jewelry. $15.00 – 25.00. Bottom: Beautiful red and pink prong-set rhinestone clip earrings in gold-tone setting. They measure 1¼" from top to bottom. Unsigned. $25.00 – 35.00.

Top: Earrings signed CONTINENTAL measure ¾" wide with prong-set green, red, and aurora borealis rhinestones encircling the center stone. Continental is a Canadian company which first opened its doors in the 1950s. $25.00 – 35.00. Bottom: Earrings with pretty green stones feature a japanned setting. The large center stone measures ⅝" in diameter. Beautiful faceted clear rhinestones encircle the center stone. Both earrings are marked ©HAR on the clip earring mechanism. $25.00 – 40.00.

Top: Prong-set clear rhinestones and black diamonds are accented with three marquis-shaped rhinestones set at an angle at the top of the earrings. Signed WARNER on the clip mechanism. $25.00 – 40.00. On either side of the middle pair of earrings are diamante chandelier earrings. Each is marked with an E in script on the earring clip mechanism. They measure 2" long. These earrings were a real find. I was attracted by the design but did not notice the faint E. The signature dates these Eisenberg clip earrings to the early 1940s. $50.00 – 75.00. Middle: Earrings with clear rhinestones, all prong-set, are signed Coro in script on screw back mechanism with no copyright symbol. $25.00 – 40.00. Bottom: Prong-set rhinestones in shiny silver-tone setting form a leaf design. They measure 1¼" long. Signed EISENBERG. $50.00 – 75.00.

Top: Star-shaped diamante earrings signed EISENBERG. $50.00 – 75.00. Middle: Prong-set aurora borealis rhinestones are featured in these petite clip style earrings. Signed KRAMER. $40.00 – 65.00. Bottom: Diamante earrings with channel-set baguettes and pear-shaped stones. Signed WARNER. $40.00 – 65.00.

Earrings

Top: Petite red and white enamel shields with top crown decoration measure 1¼" high and ¾" at widest. They are signed ©Coro on the clip mechanism. $15.00 – 25.00. Bottom: Crown earrings in an antiqued gold-tone setting feature clear and red rhinestones with faux opals. The screw-back earrings measure ⅞" x ⅞". Unsigned. $15.00 – 25.00. Crown jewelry has always been a popular motif. After the coronation of Queen Elizabeth II, crown jewelry was marketed by many jewelry companies.

Top: Copper tragedy and comedy mask earrings measure 1" high and are signed KIM on the screw-back mechanism. $20.00 – 35.00. See Figure 26 for a KIM jewelry advertisement featured in the 1960 Jewelers' Buyers Guide. Middle: Antiqued silver-tone thermoplastic Asian princess earrings. $25.00 – 35.00. Bottom: Blue plastic and white cameos in gold-tone settings have a screw-back mechanism. $10.00 – 20.00.

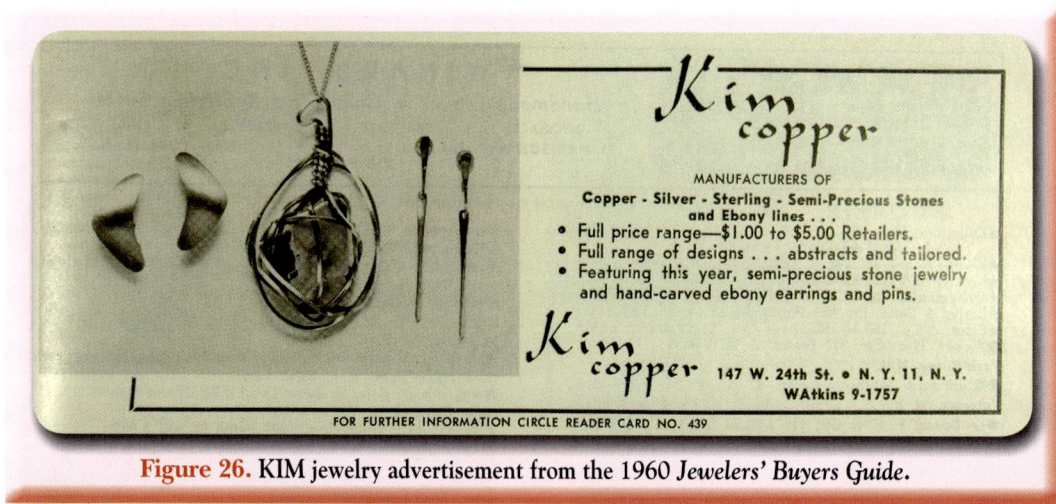

Figure 26. KIM jewelry advertisement from the 1960 *Jewelers' Buyers Guide*.

156

Children as Collectors

Sometimes in the course of browsing for jewelry, I find items other than jewelry that I just can't leave behind. The two compacts and hand mirror fit into that category. Left: Compact measuring just over 3" features enameled accents with glass stones; the powder puff is marked Dorset FIFTH AVENUE. The compact looks as if it has never been used. $150.00 – 175.00. Middle: Hand mirror has antiqued gold-tone owl with plastic turquoise accents. Note the rhinestones along the rim of the owl's eyeglasses. The owl flips up to become the handle for this clever accessory. $30.00 – 45.00. Right: Pretty compact features a jeweled royal scepter on the top. The powder puff is still in its original packing and is marked CINER. This beauty measures 2¾" across. $150.00 – 175.00.

Children as Collectors

My Daughter's Collection of Jewelry

Lower left: Graceful en pointe ballerina brooch with red rhinestones measures 2" high x 1" at its widest. Unsigned. $15.00 – 25.00. Upper right: Beautiful ballerina has pearl accents and blue rhinestones. She measures 1" x 1". Unsigned. $15.00 – 25.00.

157

Children as Collectors

Upper left: Red Lucite belly distinguishes this kitty. She also has red rhinestone eyes and long whiskers; gold-tone setting. Unsigned. $10.00 – 20.00. Middle: Gold-tone kitty has green rhinestone eyes and a moveable tail. Unsigned. $15.00 – 25.00. Lower right: Gold-tone mouse has a red Lucite belly. Unsigned. $15.00 – 25.00.

Left: Very well made enameled turtle brooch made in two pieces. It measures 2" long x 1" wide. Unsigned. $25.00 – 40.00. Upper right: Tiny green turtle stick pin has a plastic cabochon body that resembles marble. Unsigned. $10.00 – 20.00.

Left: Gold-tone walrus has turquoise cabochon eyes. It measures 1½" x 1½". Signed MONET© on a raised rectangle. $25.00 – 40.00. Right: Petite fish has a faux jade cabochon body in gold-tone setting; unsigned. $20.00 – 30.00.

Children as Collectors

Top center: Gold-tone Yorkie has a puffy tail and emerald green eyes. Signed AVON©. $15.00 – 25.00. Lower Left: Poodle pin has interesting detail on the silver-tone body. It measures 1" x 1" and is unsigned. $10.00 – 15.00. Lower right: Textured silver-tone Yorkshire terrier has bows on her ears. Pale blue rhinestone eyes provide accents. Signed GERRY'S©. $20.00 – 30.00.

Upper right: Beetle with purple stone eyes and opaque green stone trim has a faux pearl body. A tiny pin, it measures just 1" x ½". Unsigned. $15.00 – 25.00. Bottom: Pretty enameled bee brooch in a silver tone setting. This well made pin is surprisingly unsigned. It measures just 1½" x 1". $15.00 – 25.00.

Upper left: Gold-tone owl has red cabochon eyes and open-work body. It measures 1½" x ¾" and is signed ©AVON. $15.00 – 25.00. Middle: Sarah Coventry gold-tone brooch named Professor. The glasses can move up and down on the owl's face. My daughter likes this pin because she wears eyeglasses. Signed COVENTRY©. $20.00 – 30.00. Upper right: Silver-tone owl with topaz-colored rhinestone eyes and aurora borealis trim. It measures just 1" x 1". Unsigned. $10.00 – 15.00.

Children as Collectors

Left: Festive Christmas pin features a seal dressed up as Santa. This pin measures 2" x 2" and is signed ©A.J.C (for American Jewelry Chain). $20.00 – 30.00. Right: Shiny green holly leaves and red bow provide accents for this Christmas bell brooch. Note the tiny berries amongst the leaves. Unsigned. $15.00 – 25.00.

Left: Black kitty has spotted something interesting in the fish bowl made of clear Lucite. Signed ©Gold Crown Inc. $30.00 – 40.00. Right: Matte gold-tone bubble gum machine features a clear Lucite bowl with bubble gum inside. A large pin, it measures 2½" high by a little over 1" at widest. Signed A.J.C. $20.00 – 30.00.

Upper left: Pretty green frog brooch with large rose cut rhinestone body. It is signed Coro. $25.00 – 35.00. Middle: Prickly gold-tone hedgehog has green rhinestone eyes. It measures just 1½" x 1". Unsigned. $15.00 – 25.00. Upper right: Small, stylized gold-tone tiger has lots of rhinestone trim, including pavé set stones on the head and around the neck. The setting is very detailed. Signed S.A.L.© (for Swarovski). $25.00 – 40.00.

Selected Costume Jewelry Designers and Manufacturers

Left: Navy and pale blue enameled umbrella in closed position measures 2½" tall x 1" wide. Unsigned. $15.00 – 25.00. Right: Bird brooch is outlined with clear rhinestones. The bird's perch is done in black rhinestones. Every single stone is prong-set. The pin measures 2¼" x 2" at widest. Unsigned. $25.00 – 40.00.

Selected Costume Jewelry Designers and Manufacturers

This section includes a list of jewelry designers and manufacturers featured in this book. Dates of operation, signature and/or other identifying marks, and typical design characteristics are listed. The table is designed to be a summary reference for costume jewelry collectors. Keep in mind that whole volumes have been written about many of the names below. In some cases, there are many more signatures than those I have listed. What I show is a sampling of the more common signatures and marks and the ones that appeared on the jewelry in this book.

I consulted the following references including *Collecting Costume Jewelry 101* by Julia Carroll, *Amazing Gems* by Deanna Farneti Cera, *Collecting Rhinestone Colored Jewelry* by Maryanne Dolan, *Mid-century Plastic Jewelry* by Susan Maxine Klein, *Inside the Jewelry Box* by Ann Mitchell Pitman, *Costume Jewelry* by Fred Rezazadeh, *Warman's Jewelry* (3rd edition) by Christie Romero, and the following websites: www.illusionjewels.com/costumejewelrymarks.html and www.morninggloryantiques.com.

Selected Costume Jewelry Designers and Manufacturers

Manufacturer / Designer	Dates of Operation	Signature / Marks	Description / Characteristics
American Jewelry Chain, Co.	1927 – present	AJC, AJC Co., A.J.C.	There is little information available on this jewelry company; the pieces I have seen are above average figural jewelry using rhinestones and Lucite.
AMCO	1919 – late 1970s (perhaps later)	AMCO Jewels 1/20 10 K G.F. AMCO	Amco is the trademark for A. Micallef & Co. of Providence, Rhode Island, which made gold, gold-filled, and silver jewelry. They are known for elegant and classic designs.
Art, MODE-ART	1950 – 1980	ART© MODE ART©	MODE-ART was a N.Y.-based company owned by Arthur Pepper. The company marketed to wholesalers a variety of jewelry in a wide range of prices. ART designs cover almost every conceivable design including Victorian revival, whimsical figural jewelry accented with enamel and rhinestones, and Christmas jewelry.
Atwood & Sawyer	1956 – present	A&S	Atwood & Sawyer is a British company founded by Horace Atwood and his brother (Sawyer was a silent partner). They produced excellent quality jewelry easily mistaken for the real thing. They created diamante crowns for the Miss World competition. In the beginning they also created typical 1960s jewelry including Sputnik earrings and star-shaped necklaces. By the late 1980s their jewelry featured not only classic styles but some whimsical pieces decorated with oversized stones. Some A&S jewelry was made for the *Dallas* and *Dynasty* television shows.
Austria, Made in	1730 – present (most jewelry seen in the costume jewelry collectibles market is twentieth century)	AUSTRIA MADE IN AUSTRIA	Jewelry from Austria is well made with top quality rhinestones and some enameling. This jewelry rivals jewelry from the great designers in quality of materials and style. It is readily available in the collectibles market and is generally affordable. It is increasing in popularity among collectors of vintage costume jewelry.
Avon	1971 – present	©Avon E. Taylor for Avon (1993 – 1997) Barrera for Avon (1989 – 1996) K.J.L. for Avon (1986 – 2005) At least ten other signatures were used.	Avon was founded by David H. McConnell as California Perfume. The company became Avon Products, Inc. in 1939. After 1971, Avon added costume jewelry to its long list of products. They contracted with existing jewelry manufacturers such as Krementz to produce their jewelry. AVON jewelry includes some less than average quality to very well made designer pieces in a wide range of styles and materials.

Selected Costume Jewelry Designers and Manufacturers

Manufacturer / Designer	Dates of Operation	Signature / Marks	Description / Characteristics
Barclay, McClelland	1935 – 1943	McClelland Barclay At least six other signatures were used including Barclay, Barclay STERLING, and Barclay© used before 1955	McClelland jewelry is rare and extremely well made. The pieces available in the collectibles market feature top quality materials in art deco designs. It is rare to find a McClelland Barclay parure; when found they are generally expensive. McClelland designs also featured the use of sterling silver. Rice-Weiner made the jewelry for McClelland Barclay. McClelland Barclay jewelry should not be confused with Barclay, which was founded in 1946 by Alvin Rice, Robert Rice, and Louis Mark in Providence, Rhode Island, after a split with Rice-Weiner (see www.illusionjewels.com/costumejewelrymarks.html for more information).
Beatrix	1946 – 1983	BEATRIX BJ	Nat Sugarman started the Beatrix Jewelry (BJ) company in 1946 which he named after his sister Beatrice. In 1965, Beatrix jewelry was purchased by Leonard Mandell who was the company's manager. At this time they began marketing a variety of average quality Christmas trees and other Christmas jewelry including their famous Chris mouse pin.
Beau Jewels	1950s – early 1970s	Only earrings are marked BEAUJEWELS on an oval cartouche	Beau Jewels jewelry was manufactured by Bowman Foster, Inc. They made large above average rhinestone and beaded jewelry featuring unusual stones, including some with molded glass stones and lightweight construction. (Not associated with Beau-craft.)
Boucher, Marcel Boucher & Cie	1937 – 1971	MB with Phrygian cap (1937 – 1949) BOUCHER (includes inventory number) MARCEL BOUCHER MARBOUX© (registered in 1937, started using in 1955 for less expensive line) BOUCHER with name of flower for flower pins (and at least six others)	Boucher was one of the twentieth century's finest costume jewelry designers. His original and creative designs reflect the technical experience he gained while an apprentice at Cartier. His stylized rhinestone and enameled bird brooches are among his finest work. Excellent quality metalwork with high quality rhinestones are hallmarks; most jewelry is signed and includes an inventory number. See Brunialti for a table of inventory numbers and approximate dates. Boucher jewelry is sought after by collectors; some exceptional early pieces were included in the landmark Jewels of Fantasy exhibit.

Selected Costume Jewelry Designers and Manufacturers

Manufacturer / Designer	Dates of Operation	Signature / Marks	Description / Characteristics
Brand	1950s – unknown	BRAND	I could find no reliable information on jewelry marked Brand. The bracelet I have is also marked "Made in British Hong Kong." Based on the design of the piece (expandable rhinestone bracelet) jewelry marked Brand was being made in the 1950s.
Brookraft	1940s	BROOKRAFT	The only signed Brookraft jewelry I have seen features retro modern designs.
BSK	1948 – early 1980s	BSK B.S.K. B.S.K. My Fair Lady	BSK was a trademark of B. Steinberg Kaslo, and was owned by partners Julius Steinberg, Morris Kimmelman, Hyman Slovitt, Abraham Slovitt, Sanuel Friedman, and Arke, Inc. The jewelry features a variety of styles and was often gold-tone with some enameling and rhinestones accents. It is reasonably priced and readily available in the collectibles market.
Butler	unknown	BUTLER	Not Nicky Butler (contemporary jewelry signed "NB") and not Butler & Wilson (1969 – present). I was unable to find any reliable information about jewelry signed BUTLER.
Cadoro	1945 – 1980s	©CADORO Nina Ricci for CADORO (1964)	Founded by actor Steve Brody and Dan Steneskieu, a descendent of Romanian royalty who escaped his native country during WWII. Cadoro used only the best materials obtained from European suppliers. Their designs were oversized, colorful, and very well made and often featured excellent quality enameling. Their 3-D fish, animals, and Russian-inspired jewelry is highly collectible and is somewhat rare.
Calvaire	1920 – 1960	CALVAIRE Calvaire on oval cartouche Also marked with hang tags showing a bonneted woman and the legend "Le Petite Paris/Calvaire/Paris – New York"	Calvaire was founded in New York by Rachel C. Calish and Stella Aronson in the 1920s[1]. They were importers of costume jewelry and most of their items were purchased in France except during WWII when they purchased American-made goods. It is unlikely they bought jewelry from one source since the designs vary widely in structure and design; there is no Calvarire "signature look." Calvaire items include beautifully made jewelry, handbags, and compacts; the jewelry is often made with sterling. Calvaire items are extremely rare in the collectibles market. [1] Rossbacher, Nancy Dearing. Calvaire Revealed. *Vintage Fashion & Costume Jewelry*, Vol. 17, No. 3, 2007.

Selected Costume Jewelry Designers and Manufacturers

Manufacturer / Designer	Dates of Operation	Signature / Marks	Description / Characteristics
Capri	1952 – 1977	CAPRI with © after 1955	Capri was owned by Sol Smith. The jewelry was very well made and featured colored rhinestones and pearls in interesting and dimensional designs. Jewelry marked with CAPRI without © was made between 1952 – 1955. Some Capri designs were produced by Florenza.
Carl-Art, Inc.	1936 – 1976	The initials "CA" with an arrow through it.	Founded in 1937 in Providence, Rhode Island, Carl-Art was owned by Arthur Loercher and Carl Schraysshuen. The company made jewelry in smaller, classic designs, some featuring rhinestones, sterling, and gold-filled fittings. They sold under their own name and also made jewelry for other companies including Walter Lampl. Carl died in 1953 and his wife sold their half of the company.
Carnegie, Hattie	1918 – 1979	HC in a diamond HATTIE CARNEGIE on an oval cartouche Carnegie Double Exposure Miss Hattie and at least ten more	Born Henrietta Kanengeiser in Vienna in 1886, Hattie's "rags to riches" life story is remarkable. Her jewelry was originally made to complement her fashions; early pieces included lavalieres, shoe buckles, scarf clips, and hair ornaments. Her highly collectible figural jewelry includes rams, fish, elephants, Asian themes, and Egyptian revival designs. She also marketed softer, feminine designs with pearls and rhinestones. Carnegie's first costume jewelry was made after 1939. The company was acquired by Chromalloy American Corp. in 1976, however the Carnegie name was still being used in 1978. All of her jewelry styles are collectible; the figural jewelry is especially popular with collectors.
Carolee	1972 – present	CAROLEE©	Founded by Carolee Friedlander in 1972, Carolee jewelry is best known for copies of the Duchess of Windsor jewels, including the famous flamingo pin. Carolee jewelry is well made with high quality materials including faux pearls and clear and colored rhinestones in silver and gold-tone settings. The Carolee company was purchased by Retail Brand Alliance in 2001. Her Duchess copies are the most collectible of Carolee jewelry and are rarely seen in the collectibles market.

Selected Costume Jewelry Designers and Manufacturers

Manufacturer / Designer	Dates of Operation	Signature / Marks	Description / Characteristics
Castlecliff	1918 – 1977	CASTLECLIFF STERLING CASTLECLIFF CASTLEMARK (1948 – 1952) Anne Klein for Castlecliff (1977)	Castlecliff was founded in 1918 by Clifford Furst and Joseph Bobley. They began marketing their jewelry after a court battle with Brier MFG. Co. over design patents. One of their company slogans was "the talked about jewelry." Castlecliff jewelry is very well made using excellent materials including rhinestones and faux gemstones (faux jade and turquoise) in heavy gold-tone settings. Egyptian revival themes are common in their later jewelry.
Caviness, Alice	1945 – 1990s	ALICE CAVINESS on oval cartouche ALICE CAVINESS Sterling Germany ALICE CAVINESS Sterling A.C. with metal content	Caviness jewelry was designed to complement her fashions. Ms. Caviness even had her own jewelry factory. The business continued after her death in 1983. Her designs are large and bold, and employ high quality materials including decorative stones. Not all Alice Caviness jewelry was signed. It is also somewhat rare in the collectibles market.
Celebrity	1970s	CELEBRITY N.Y. CELEBRITY ©Celebrity Celebrity® or marked with hang tags	Celebrity jewelry located at 34th St. Brooklyn, New York, was sold through home parties and featured a variety of classic and contemporary styles.
Ceno[2] [2] I thought the mark might be "Geno" which was a division of Richelieu. However, the type of jewelry sold under the Geno mark was not signed but identified with a hang tag.	unknown	Ceno©	I was unable to find any reliable information on this company. I have only occasionally seen pieces of Ceno jewelry in the collectibles market; the pieces I have seen have a © symbol.
Cerrito Jewelry LTD.	1977 – present	Cerrito©	I was unable to find any reliable information on this company. I have only occasionally seen pieces of jewelry marked "Cerrito" in the collectibles market; the pieces I have seen have a © symbol.
Ciner	1892 – present first costume jewelry was made in 1931	CINER MC on a raised rectangle CINER® and at least five more.	Ciner features high quality jewelry that often appeared to be the real thing, Ciner pieces feature beautiful designs made with rows of tiny rhinestones, faux turquoise, and pearls, combined with superior metalwork. Only Ciner jewelry produced after WWII is marked. Interestingly, after the Boucher firm was sold, Sandra Boucher worked for a time as a designer for Ciner.

Selected Costume Jewelry Designers and Manufacturers

Manufacturer / Designer	Dates of Operation	Signature / Marks	Description / Characteristics
Colco	1950s – 1960s	COLCO©	I could find no reliable information on dates and manufacturer of jewelry marked COLCO. Based on jewelry currently available in the collectibles market, COLCO jewelry was Asian-themed, elaborate, and well made. Unsigned pieces are often confused with HAR, SELRO, SELINI, and Hobé. I have never seen a signed piece of Colco jewelry without the © symbol.
Continental	1950s – unknown	CONTINENTAL	Continental is a Canadian company; their well made jewelry features classic designs with rhinestones and pearls. It appears infrequently in the collectibles market.
Coro	1901 – 1979	Coro used many signatures; a few of the more commonly occurring ones are: Coro Coro Craft (1933 – 1979) Francois© (1938 – 1950s) Pegasus symbol used after WWII Vendome (See Vendome)	Coro is probably the hardest to describe in just a paragraph or two. Coro jewelry used at least 50 different trademarks between 1930 – 1960 but Coro, Coro Craft, and Coro Duette are among the most significant. Emanuel Cohn and Carl Rosenberger opened the Coro factory in Providence, Rhode Island, in 1929 and became the largest manufacturer of affordable and accessible costume jewelry in the U.S. Adolf Katz was a major force behind Coro's designs. Coro employed an outstanding team of designers including Selwyn Young who later joined Lisner; Gene and Reno Verrecchio (Verri), who later founded Gem-Craft; and Anthony Aquilino. Over its long history, Coro jewelry featured a wide variety of designs including figural jewelry with plastic bodies (jelly bellies), crowns, beautifully enameled flower brooches (some en tremblant), sterling silver, and combination rhinestone/thermoplastic parures.
Craft, Gem-Craft	1948 – present	CRAFT Jewelcraft (the Jewelcraft mark was first used by Coro in 1920; it is now owned by Gem-Craft. They renewed it in 2002).	Craft is a signature of Gem-Craft which is owned by Ron and Gene Verrecchio (Verri). Gene also designed jewelry for KJL, Capri, Mandle, Tancer, Kramer, and Cadoro, and worked as a head designer for Coro for over 31 years with many famous designs to his credit. Gem-Craft jewelry is very well made and features faux pearls, cabochons of faux gems, and enameled designs in gold-tone settings. Gem-Craft was originally called Craftsman. The Jewelcraft mark first used by Coro is now owned by Gem-Craft.

Selected Costume Jewelry Designers and Manufacturers

Manufacturer / Designer	Dates of Operation	Signature / Marks	Description / Characteristics
Czechoslovakia	Most of the Czech jewelry in today's collectible market was made between 1918 and 1938	CZECH Czechoslovakia (two of many marks used)	Costume jewelry made in Czechoslovakia often features distinctive Victorian revival and Art Deco designs. This jewelry is made with high quality rhinestones, molded and faceted glass beads, and colored glass that was cut to look like real gemstones. Czech jewelry is often marked in hard to see places, including on a brooch stem or the side of a catch, the back of a necklace clasp, or on the safety catch. Czech silver jewelry is marked with a woman's head with a scarf or bonnet or a rabbit or goat head (after 1955).
Dalsheim	1930s – 1978	DALSHEIM White Jet Also identified with hang tags	The company was founded by Maurice Dalsheim in the late 1930s. Most jewelry was not signed and was marked only with a hang tag. Their jewelry featured seed pearls and glass and plastic beads. Dalsheim also made small gold-tone novelty pins, some with enamelwork, in Victorian revival styles. Dalsheim jewelry is rare in the collectibles market.
DeLizza & Elster, Inc.	1947 – 1990 1967 – 1968 designed and sold "Juliana" line	Marked with hang tags only "Juliana Original" used for about two years. Other names used: Mystic Jewelry Greenwood Designs Judy, Judy, Judy Fifth Avenue Accessories	DeLizza & Elster was founded by William DeLizza and Harold Elster in New York City. In 1967 – 1968 D&E designed, produced, and marketed Juliana jewelry (named after Frank DeLizza's mother). However, they mainly made jewelry for others including Weiss, Kramer, Hobé, Eisenberg, more contemporary companies like Talbot's and Ann Taylor. Juliana jewelry has distinctive design characteristics including a five-link design on bracelets, beautiful center stones with open backs, navette rhinestones with unfoiled, open backs, and excellent workmanship. Juliana jewelry is readily available in the collectible market; however, the demand for this beautifully made jewelry has caused prices to escalate. Expect to pay $900 and up for a parure. Jewelry in some of their original designs is currently being offered by Frank DeLizza, son of William.
De Nicola	1957 – 1970	DE NICOLA on oval cartouche or raised rectangle	De Nicola jewelry is rare and beautifully made using high quality materials in oversized and fabulous designs. Jerry De Nicola Inc. of New York marketed this jewelry. Their slogan was the "real look." It is somewhat rare in the collectibles market; De Nicola figural pieces are sought by collectors.

Selected Costume Jewelry Designers and Manufacturers

Manufacturer / Designer	Dates of Operation	Signature / Marks	Description / Characteristics
Doddz	1952 – 1977	DODDS© DODDZ	Jewel Creations, a subsidiary of William Doddz and Company, was based in Newark, New Jersey, beginning in 1952. Their primary product was home-craft kits for making jewelry, The designs featured gold-tone and silver-tone in classic designs, including Christmas themes, and often used colored rhinestones.
Eisenberg	1935 – present	EISENBERG (in block letters 1945 – 1958) Eisenberg Original (1935 – 1945) Sterling (1943 – 1948) E in script (1942 – 1945) Eisenberg Ice© first used in 1935. Many Eisenberg pieces were unsigned	Founded by Jonas Eisenberg in Chicago, to initially sell ready-to-wear fashions. The first Eisenberg jewelry was designed to complement their clothes and was sold as part of the fashion ensemble. These early jewelry pieces were unsigned. The popularity of the jewelry was undeniable; store owners reported that the brooches were disappearing from the clothes! Jonas's son, Sam, began to sell jewelry separately from their fashions and by 1958, Eisenberg was out of the fashion business altogether. Eisenberg jewelry remains a favorite among collectors because it consistently employed high quality clear and colored rhinestones in hand settings, including sterling silver. In the 1970s Eisenberg produced a series of enameled jewelry that was influenced by modern artists including Braques, Calder, Chagall, Picasso, and Miró. In 1994 and again in 2000, Eisenberg issued a classic series featuring remakes of classic designs. These are highly collectible and were marked "Eisenberg Ice." Unfortunately as prices started to escalate, Eisenberg fakes flooded the collectibles market; even experienced collectors were fooled by the copies.

169

Selected Costume Jewelry Designers and Manufacturers

Manufacturer / Designer	Dates of Operation	Signature / Marks	Description / Characteristics
Elzac	1941 – 1947	Marked with hang tags ELZAC Made in California	Elzac was founded by Zachary Zemby, H. Weiss, Z. Taubes, and A. Oben in Los Angeles. Elzac Inc. produced large, creative novelty jewelry during WWII. They used ceramic, Lucite, feathers, wood, felt, and other materials during a period when conventional jewelry materials were scarce. Elzac jewelry was made by hand and unsigned, except for a hang tag or label. Designs included animals and exotic faces, some with elaborate headdresses. Many Elzac designs were patented by E. Handler (of Barbie doll fame) so it is easy for collectors to research original designs. Some jewelry similar to Elzac is often and incorrectly attributed to Elzac, including green ceramic heads with copper backing. The popularity of Elzac jewelry, including the whimsical "Victim of Fashion" brooches, has been steadily increasing and prices are rising.
Emmons	1949 – 1981	©EMMONS Emmolite Em J	Charles Stuart founded Emmons in Newark, New York; he named the company after his wife, Caroline Emmons. Stuart also founded Sarah Coventry eight months later. Emmons jewelry is of average quality and features a variety of designs including colored rhinestones in gold-tone settings. Emmons jewelry is found less frequently than Sarah Coventry jewelry.
Eugene	1952 – 1962	Eugene on an oval cartouche	Eugene Schultz made top quality jewelry in the tradition of Miriam Haskell. Some Eugene jewelry is not signed. Eugene Schultz died in 1964. All of his pieces were his own design and employed materials including seed pearls and colored cabochons in ornate and complex designs. Eugene jewelry was only produced for about 10 years; it is rare in the collectibles market.

Selected Costume Jewelry Designers and Manufacturers

Manufacturer / Designer	Dates of Operation	Signature / Marks	Description / Characteristics
Florenza	1950 – 1981	FLORENZA© (Used the © before 1955) Rosenfeld for FLORENZA	Dan Kasoff Inc. first produced jewelry in the 1930s. The Florenza name was first used in 1948. Kasoff started his own company which he named after his wife Florence. They also manufactured jewelry for other companies including Kramer, Capri, and Estee Lauder. Florenza jewelry is very well made and included Victorian revival designs with antiqued settings and high quality, unusual stones that mimic the real thing. Florenza perfected three finishes including French gold, French rose, and Wedgwood. They also produced accessory items, including some for Estee Lauder. Florenza jewelry is extremely popular among collectors and is still reasonably priced.
Garné	1945 – 1960s	GARNE	Garné jewelry is average quality, employing classic diamante designs, some in an Art Deco style. Garné also made watch fobs and chatelaines. This jewelry is not commonly found in the collectibles market.
Germany, West	1949 – 1990	Made in Germany West Made in West Germany Western Germany Western Germany U.S. Zone Germany (before 1949 or after 1990)	Jewelry made in West Germany is highly stylized, ornate, and reminiscent of Victorian designs. It is common to see elaborate filigree settings with cameos, colored cabochons, pearls, and other faux gemstones. It is nicely designed average quality jewelry and is usually moderately priced.
Gerry's	1950 – mid 1990s	GERRY'S©	Gerry's jewelry is average quality, highly stylized novelty pins of animals including dogs, cats, and mice. Designs include gold-tone and silver-tone pieces, usually smaller jewelry, using colored rhinestones. It is readily available in the collectibles market.
Givenchy	1952 – present	GIVENCHY PARIS on an oval cartouche GIVENCHY PARIS NEW YORK	Givenchy designs are classic and usually large scale using gold plating, Lucite, and other plastics. Hubert de Givenchy began his career in 1945 designing for Schiaparelli; he opened his own shop in 1952.
Goldette	1958 – mid-1970s	GOLDETTE Goldette N.Y.© ©Goldette Goldette®	Goldette is the trademark name of Circle jewelry company which was owned by Ben Gartner and son Michael. Well made Victorian revival styles are hallmarks of Goldette jewelry. They emphasized metalwork with enamel and intaglio accents, and incorporated faux turquoise, pearls, and other imitation stones to provide accents in their designs.

Selected Costume Jewelry Designers and Manufacturers

Manufacturer / Designer	Dates of Operation	Signature / Marks	Description / Characteristics
Gold Crown, Inc.	? – present	GOLD CROWN INC	Gold Crown, Inc. and Central Novelty Company are located at 403 Charles St., Providence, Rhode Island. They are listed as manufacturers, importers, and exporters of costume jewelry, fine jewelry, imitation jewelry, and jewelry-making tools and supplies.
Graziano, Robert J.	Late 1970s – present	R.J. GRAZIANO GRAZIANO	Graziano jewelry is large, glamorous, finely crafted costume jewelry with a vintage look. It includes interesting details; gold and silver plate and copper base metals with clear and colored rhinestones. Graziano has also marketed a line of handbags and belts. This jewelry is sold through a home shopping network.
Green, Judith	1960s – unknown	JUDITH GREEN on a cartouche	Judith Green jewelry includes better quality rhinestone and gold-tone pieces and includes whimsical figural jewelry, scarf clips, and belts. I can find no other reliable information except that, based on vintage ads I have seen, it was sold in better department stores in the 1960s.
Hagler, Stanley	1953 – 1996	STANLEY HAGLER N.Y.C. STANLEY HAGLER on an oval cartouche	Stanley Hagler graduated from the University of Denver Law School but went on to create costume jewelry beginning in 1951 in Greenwich Village, New York. By 1968 his breathtaking creations were achieving worldwide recognition and he was recognized by the Great Designs in Costume Jewelry program. His large, bold, hand wrought designs are sought after by collectors who are willing to pay hundreds of dollars for a single piece.
Halbe	1950s – 1963	HALBE	Halbe Jewelry Co. was located at 411 5th Avenue in New York. It is rare and hard to find. It is usually high quality and features rhinestones and enameled designs. Designs include some figural jewelry as well.

Selected Costume Jewelry Designers and Manufacturers

Manufacturer / Designer	Dates of Operation	Signature / Marks	Description / Characteristics
HAR	1950s – 1960s	HAR with a copyright symbol	HAR is one of the great mysteries that costume jewelry sleuths have yet to solve. HAR jewelry is known for excellent enameling and fantastic figural jewelry, beautifully detailed Oriental figures with imitation ivory faces, genies, cobras, dragons, and blackamoors; also enameled fruit, small whimsical animals, and extremely well made jewelry with imitation pearls and rhinestones. In some references, I have seen HAR referred to as Hargo (Hargo Jewelry Co. is listed in the 1960 *Jewelers' Buyers Guide* with an address of 82 Canal Street in New York). Selected pieces of HAR jewelry were featured in the Jewels of Fantasy exhibit propelling this jewelry to international fame. HAR jewelry is highly collectible and sought after by collectors. It can be extremely expensive, especially the cobra, genie, and dragon pieces.
Haskell, Miriam	1926 – present	Early Haskell pieces were not signed; the rarest mark is a horseshoe-shaped plaque bearing her name in capital letters (late 1940s). In the 1950s her name appears on an oval cartouche; also MIRIAM HASKELL on oval hang tag	Miriam Haskell jewelry typically features masses of seed pearls, rich filigree metalwork with an antique patina, and a mixture of interesting stones. Her jewelry is always backed with an openwork filigree metal plate. It has a decidedly feminine look and is well made; Miriam Haskell vintage ads featuring Haskell jewelry are among the finest and most artistic of all vintage jewelry advertisements. Haskell jewelry is extremely popular with collectors. Frank Hess, Larry Vrba, and Millie Petronzio all designed for Haskell.
Hobé Cie Limited	1915 – 1995 (Jewelry marked Hobé is still being made; however the original company found by the Hobé family is defunct.)	©Hobé Hobé in a crown Hobé with crossed swords Hobé with metal content Some pieces were dated (1957 – 1965) Several other marks were used.	Begun by Jacques Hobé in Paris in 1887, the company was brought to America by Jacques's son William in 1915. They brought traditional methods to the production of their unique costume jewelry which was sold at upscale stores. Hobé jewelry is well known for romantic floral brooches and their Jewels of Legendary Splendor from the 1940s and 1950s which feature elaborate settings and cascading rhinestones. Hobé is also noted for excellently made figural jewelry. William's grandson was running the company when it was sold in 2000.

Selected Costume Jewelry Designers and Manufacturers

Manufacturer / Designer	Dates of Operation	Signature / Marks	Description / Characteristics
Hollycraft	1938 – 1971	HOLLYCRAFT & date (first used around 1950) HOLLYCRAFT COPR. & date (after 1955) Also marked with hang tags Early jewelry was not marked	Joseph Chorbajian, a survivor of the Turkish massacre, emigrated to the U.S. in 1917 where he founded the Hollywood Jewelry Mfg. Company in New York in 1938. The jewelry was known for antique finishes and colorful pastel stones of varying sizes in a variety of beautiful and well constructed designs. Early Hollycraft jewelry was unmarked; later jewelry was clearly marked with name and date. Signed and dated Hollycraft jewelry is sought after by collectors. Hollycraft also made jewelry for Kramer, PaKula, and Weiss.
Hong Kong	1940s – present	HONG KONG	Hong Kong jewelry was made before WWII through the early 1950s and again after the Korean War. It varies in quality; some is above average and some below. Multi-strand necklaces feature fancy clasps with glass, faux pearls, and pretty art beads. Also available in the collectibles market are rhinestone expansion bracelets. Collectors favor plastic fruit and flower necklace and bracelet sets. During the 1980s some of the best fake pearls came from Hong Kong.
Iskin, Harry	1930s – 1953	Cartouche marked with Iskin or logo (Larger Capital I intersecting capital H) Mark includes metal content (1/20 12 KGF)	A common theme in Iskin jewelry is floral motifs using Art Deco designs. The jewelry also includes Victorian revival and retro modern styles; some glass stones, pearls, curlicues, ribbons, leaves, and stamped metal components. It is rare in the collectibles market.
Japan	After 1945	Made in Japan (after 1952) Occupied Japan (1945 – 1952)	Jewelry made in Japan is known for the use of inexpensive beads and matching earrings; also celluloid figural jewelry which is gaining popularity in the collectibles market after being mentioned in recently published books on collectible plastic jewelry.
Jeanne	1950s – 1960s	JEANNE©	Jeanne jewelry is well made and features whimsical figural pieces with rhinestones and beads, some pieces en tremblant. Little is known about this mark which is seen infrequently in the collectibles market. Jeanne jewelry was mentioned in *Seventeen* magazine in 1962 – 1963. I have only seen Jeanne jewelry with the © symbol.

Selected Costume Jewelry Designers and Manufacturers

Manufacturer / Designer	Dates of Operation	Signature / Marks	Description / Characteristics
Jonette Jewelry Company	1943 – 2006	J.J. (first used in 1970) Artifacts first used in 1986	J.J. is the mark of Jonette Jewelry Co. of Providence, Rhode Island, founded by Abraham Lisker in 1943. It was first called the Providence Jewelry Co. During WWII they ceased operations and then started again with the name Jonette (name comes from Lisker's parents John and Etta). Jonette jewelry is known mostly for figural pins and Christmas jewelry.
Joseff of Hollywood	1938 – present	JOSEFF HOLLYWOOD JOSEFF Joseff (recent productions use this mark)	Joseff of Hollywood made historically accurate jewelry for Hollywood films during the 1930s – 1940s. He perfected a matte finish that did not interfere with bright studio lights. He rented his jewelry to movie studios rather than sell it outright; as a result he amassed a huge archive. In 1938 Joseff started a commercial line which was sold in the best stores and was very popular. It was collected by Joan Crawford and other high profile actresses. His jewelry was extremely well made with excellent materials and included both traditional and less conventional subjects. After his untimely death in 1948, his wife, Joan Castle, continued to operate the business. In the 1990s, some newly assembled Joseff jewelry designs have been introduced into the collectibles market using older, authentic fittings.
Judy Lee	1949 – 1980s	JUDY LEE Judy Lee Judy Lee Jewels	Judy Lee jewelry was produced by the Blanchette company based in Chicago and sold through home parties. It featured interesting designs with pearls, rhinestones, intaglio cameos, and other interesting stones. Judy Lee jewelry is becoming increasingly popular in the collectibles market, in particular the rhinestone pieces.
Karu	1940 – mid 1970s	Karu KARU Fifth Avenue Karu Arke, Inc KARU ARKE, INC Karu STERLING	Karu was made by Kaufman & Ruderman, Inc. The jewelry featured mostly traditional rhinestone sets similar to Weiss and Kramer; they also made some Victorian revival jewelry. Karu jewelry made during the 1960s has a distinctly "mod" look. It is readily available in the collectibles market.
Kim	1956 – ?	KIM without ©	Kim Copper, located at 147 W. 24th St. in New York, manufactured copper, silver, sterling, semi-precious, and ebony jewelry lines in a variety of styles — "abstracts and tailored." Kim jewelry was featured in the 1960 *Jewelers' Buyers Guide*. The jewelry was above average quality and moderately priced at the time it was sold. Now it is rarely found in the collectibles market.

Selected Costume Jewelry Designers and Manufacturers

Manufacturer / Designer	Dates of Operation	Signature / Marks	Description / Characteristics
Kramer	1943 – 1980	KRAMER KRAMER of N.Y. KRAMER of NEW YORK Dior by KRAMER Amourelle (by Frank Hess who joined Kramer sometime after he left Haskell) KRAMER STERLING MADE IN AUSTRIA & KRAMER The Diamond Look	Louis Kramer founded Kramer in 1943; he was later joined by his brothers Morris and Harry. Kramer jewelry features excellent quality rhinestone pieces, some with icing similar to that found on Eisenberg and Weiss jewelry. Louis also designed jewelry which included more casual thermoplastic pieces and pretty enameled designs. The © symbol is not useful for dating because it was not used after 1955.
Krementz	1866 – present Started making costume jewelry in the 1950s — no costume jewelry made after 1997	KREMENTZ (did not use ©) KREMENTZ USA And at least six others	Krementz was established in 1866. As the market evolved, so too did their products. They went from collar buttons and cuff links to finely made costume jewelry by the 1950s. Krementz jewelry employed excellent quality materials. Their signature look is delicate with the appearance of fine jewelry because they routinely used 10K and 14K gold plating when making costume jewelry. Their classic designs changed very little over the years. Fine jewelry is still being made and is signed "Richard Krementz Gemstones."
Laguna	1944 – 1980s	LAGUNA KJL Laguna	Made by Royal Craftsman, Inc., in New York (founded by Louis & Lillian Detkin) Laguna jewelry usually features multi-strand necklaces with matching earrings. Materials used include crystal and plastic beads and pearls.

Selected Costume Jewelry Designers and Manufacturers

Manufacturer / Designer	Dates of Operation	Signature / Marks	Description / Characteristics
Lane, Kenneth J.	1963 – present	K.J.L. (1960s – 1970s) KJL Kenneth Jay Lane Kenneth Lane© KJL for Avon (1986 – present)	Kenneth J. Lane began his career by designing shoes and the rest is history. His jewelry designs were inspired by his travels and employed a variety of unusual and high quality materials. He was famous for copying the precious jewels of the rich and famous. His jewelry is of excellent quality and over his 40+ year career, almost every conceivable design, from classical to whimsical, has appeared. His early pieces are especially collectible and command high prices when they can be found. He also designed jewelry for Avon from 1986 to 2004.
La Roco	1918 – unknown	Only earrings signed LA ROCO La Roco	La Roco was started by Layko, Ross & Co., Inc. The jewelry was well made using high quality materials, including colorful rhinestones, in large, shiny gold-tone settings. La Roco jewelry is rare in the collectibles market. Considering its rarity and quality of construction, it is reasonably priced when it can be found.
Ledo (Polcini)	1911 – 1980s	Ledo (1948 – 1963) In the early 1960s, renamed POLCINI Lee Menichi for Polcini (1971)	Polcini jewelry was founded by Ralph Polcini and was made by the Leading Jewelry Manufacturing company. They made high quality diamante designs and also used colored stones in beautiful and classic designs. Polcini jewelry is typical of 1960s designs and features rhinestones and rhodium settings.
Les Bernard	1962 – 1996	LES BERNARD LES BERNARD, INC. LES BERNARD STERLING	Les Bernard Jewelry company was founded by Bernard Shapiro and Lester Joy in 1962. Bernard is the son of Harold Shapiro who founded the Vogue Jewelry Co. and Lester Joy was a designer. Like Atwood & Sawyer, Les Bernard manufactured jewelry for the *Dynasty* TV series. They also made jewelry for Mary McFadden, James Galanos, and Ugo Correani. Their jewelry features very well made rhinestone pieces in a variety of designs; they have also made hand-knotted pearl necklaces. The jewelry is well constructed and high quality.

Selected Costume Jewelry Designers and Manufacturers

Manufacturer / Designer	Dates of Operation	Signature / Marks	Description / Characteristics
Lisner	1904 – mid-1980s	Lisner mark first used in 1938 LISNER LISNER© Lisner Lisner and at least nine other marks	The D. Lisner Company, was founded in New York in 1904. They did not own their own factory; their jewelry was made by others including Whiting & Davis. Until the 1930s much of Lisner's jewelry was imported from Europe and sold wholesale. Lisner imported Schiaparelli jewelry and marketed it in the U.S. prior to WWII. In the 1930s Lisner teamed with Urie Mandle (father of Robert Mandle of the R. Mandle Co.) to build a retail, domestically produced jewelry line in Providence, Rhode Island. In the 1970s, Richelieu and Lisner became one company and renamed Lisner-Richelieu. Lisner was acquired in 1979 by Victoria Creations (also known as Victoria & Co.). Today the company is owned by the Jones Apparel Group. Many Lisner designs feature translucent plastic leaves which may have been imported from Europe. Jewelry produced in the 1950s and 1960s featured timeless designs including leaves, fruits, and flowers. Lisner thermoplastic parures are extremely popular among vintage jewelry collectors and can sometimes cost several hundred dollars, depending on the design.
Liz Claiborne	1976 – present	LC Liz Claiborne, Inc. LCI	Liz Claiborne designs feature a variety of jewelry from gold-tone with rhinestones, seed pearls, turquoise, and faux coral cabochons to more classically designed jewelry. Monet Group, Inc. including Trifari and Marvella was bought by Liz Claiborne in 2000; their production has moved overseas.
Mamselle	Early 1950s – 1999	MAMSELLE first used in June 1962; MAMSELLE with Eiffel Tower symbol first used in Jan. 1968	The company was started by B.B. Greenberg in Providence, Rhode Island. In 1999, they petitioned to have the trademark removed from the books. Mamselle jewelry is average quality and was inexpensive to purchase when it was first made. Enameled figural designs are commonly seen.

Selected Costume Jewelry Designers and Manufacturers

Manufacturer / Designer	Dates of Operation	Signature / Marks	Description / Characteristics
Marvella	1911 – present	MARVELLA© Marvella and many more	Marvella jewelry was manufactured by Weinreich Brothers Company in Philadelphia, Pennsylvania. They made jewelry for many other companies as well. They are probably best known for their well made faux pearl jewelry. They also made popular figural jewelry and crystal necklaces. In the early 1980s they were purchased by Crystal Brands Jewelry Group, which included Monet and Trifari. In 2000 they were purchased by Liz Claiborne, Inc. Jewelry using the Marvella name is still being produced but manufacturing has moved out of the U.S.
Mazer/Jomaz	1923 – 1981	MAZER BROS. (1926 – 1951) MAZER (1946 – 1981) JOMAZ (1946 – 1981) MAZER Sterling Also used at least five other marks	In 1923, Joseph Mazer, a Russian immigrant, and his brother Lincoln founded Mazer Bros. in New York. They began making costume jewelry by 1927; among Mazer master designers was Marcel Boucher. Mazer consistently used high quality materials to make well constructed jewelry. In 1946 the brothers split off into Joseph Mazer Co. (Jomaz) and Mazer Bros. Joseph's company was in business until 1981; Lincoln's until 1951. Their timeless and elegant designs are popular with collectors. Jomaz figural jewelry is rare and highly collectible. Expect to pay several hundred dollars for a Mazer parure.
Mexico	1940 – present	Mexico 925 (after 1947)	During WWII when costume jewelry materials were in short supply, some companies (including Eisenberg) contracted with Mexican silversmiths to make jewelry. At the same time, jewelry designed and made by Mexican silversmiths also became popular. Much of this jewelry was made in an area of Mexico called Taxco. Since it is still being made and signed Taxco and 925, the presence of either of these marks is not necessarily helpful in dating the jewelry. Earlier jewelry has an eagle stamp with a number. Jewelry made after 1979 is marked with the initials of the silversmith and also a number indicating the silversmith's position on a registry.

Selected Costume Jewelry Designers and Manufacturers

Manufacturer / Designer	Dates of Operation	Signature / Marks	Description / Characteristics
Mimi Di Niscemi	1962 – 1970s	MIMI d N© date on raised rectangle or cartouche	A graduate of the Philadelphia Museum School and School of Applied Arts in Paris, Ms. Di Niscemi set up a company in 1962 in New York. She designed and produced jewelry and also established an archive of designs. Her elaborate designs employed pearls, colored cabochons, and rhinestones in interesting and ornate settings. In 1968, she won one of 35 prizes offered by the Great Designers in Costume Jewelry Awards sponsored by D. Swarovski. Mimi Di Niscemi jewelry is rare in the collectibles marked; it is noteworthy for its excellent design, craftsmanship, and materials.
Miracle	1946 – present	Various signatures including MIRACLE, MIRACLE followed by BRITAIN CELTIC JEWELRY and at least ten other signatures	Although several American manufacturers used the Miracle trademark, Miracle jewelry commonly found in the collectibles market today is made by A. Hill & Co., Birmingham, England, and refers to jewelry set in silver-tone metal with a finish designed to emulate pewter. It also has multicolored agate stones in traditional designs. Miracle made some sterling and figural pieces; the figural jewelry is rare and very collectible. It is moderately priced except for the figural jewelry which can be expensive.
Monet	1929 – present	MONET Monet MONET 2 MONET STERLING Monocraft MONET Jewelers	Monocraft Products, Co. was founded in 1929 by Jay and Michael Chernow in Providence, Rhode Island. By 1937 they were making jewelry sets which were mostly modern gold-tone and silver-tone designs, some with pearl and rhinestone accents, and Christmas jewelry. The company was sold several times and finally acquired by Liz Claiborne, Inc. in 2000.
Mylu	1960s – 1970	MYLU©	Most Mylu jewelry consists of stylized Christmas jewelry and small figural pins. Lynne Gordon and Marge Borofsky founded the company which became a division of Coro in 1968; in the 1970s Lynne and Marge joined Tancer II.
Napier	1875 – 1999	NAPIER named first used in 1922 © used after 1955 NAPIER Sterling Napier And at least eighteen others	Napier was founded in 1875 by Whitney & Rice in North Attleboro, Massachusetts. The line includes a wide variety of designs over many years including several classic designs in well made, traditional gold-tone or silver-tone. Napier charm bracelets are highly collectible.

Selected Costume Jewelry Designers and Manufacturers

Manufacturer / Designer	Dates of Operation	Signature / Marks	Description / Characteristics
Newhouse	1950s – 1960s	NEWHOUSE	Newhouse was the company of J.J. Newhouse and Son, Inc. They made above average rhinestone and pearl jewelry. Jewelry marked NEWHOUSE is rare in the collectibles market.
PAM	Possibly 1950s – 1960s	PAM©	Like many companies of the 1950s – 1960s, little is known about this jewelry. Pam jewelry is of average quality construction with above average designs including exotic silver-tone and gold-tone figural pieces with rhinestones. Pam designs can also be found in more traditional rhinestone designs and thermoplastic jewelry. It has been suggested that PAM may have been started by a French designer named Pierre Anston Masson but this information is not verified.
Panetta	1945 – 1995	©PANETTA	Panetta was started by Benedetto Panetto in Naples, Italy, where he made hand-crafted platinum jewelry. After coming to the U.S., he became the chief model-maker for Trifari. When Trifari moved to Providence in the 1930s, Panetta stayed in New York City with the Pennino brothers. After WWII he established his own company with his sons Amadeo and Armand. They made original designs hand-set in sterling silver and later worked in white metal using gold and rhodium for a two-tone effect. Panetta was known for the "real look" in fine costume jewelry; their line includes very well made enameled and rhinestone jewelry. The company continued under the management of Benedetta's sons Amadeo and Armand. It was purchased by a foreign company in the 1980s.
Park Lane, Jewels by	1955 – present	PARKLANE on oval cartouche Jewels by Park Lane (with crown)	The company was founded by Arthur and Shirley LeVin in Chicago, Illinois. Park Lane jewelry is sold using direct sales/in-home marketing. They make a variety of average and above-average pearl and gold-tone jewelry, some featuring rhinestones and interesting plastic designs.
Pastelli	1950s – 1980s	PASTELLI Pastelli® Pastelli©	Royal of Pittsburgh, Pennsylvania, made Pastelli jewelry. Their signature look was pretty pastel enameled jewelry in classic and modern designs. Pastelli also made more traditional rhinestone and gold-tone jewelry in classic designs. It is somewhat rare in the collectibles market and is moderately priced.

Selected Costume Jewelry Designers and Manufacturers

Manufacturer / Designer	Dates of Operation	Signature / Marks	Description / Characteristics
Pell	1941 – present	PELL ©PELL	Founded by brothers Bill, Tony, Joe, and Alfred Gaita, early Pell designs featured mostly clear rhinestones. Their elegant and high quality jewelry includes unique and unusual figural pins in shiny rhodium settings. Alfred continues in his Brooklyn factory making tailored gold jewelry and gold with pearls.
Polcini (see Ledo)			
Rebajes	1932 – 1967	Rebajes Crafts NYC Rebajes Rebajes STERLING	Francisco Rebajes was born in 1906 in the Dominican Republic. He studied briefly in Barcelona, Spain, and then moved to New York in 1923. He eventually became a successful artist and by 1937, his work was recognized at the Paris Exposition Universelle. He turned to jewelry making and his upscale New York salon became a popular meeting place. He returned to Spain where he continued to make jewelry until his death in 1990. His modern, nonobjective sculptural designs rendered in copper have a distinctive look. His status was elevated to that of "studio artist" after his work was included in the Messengers of Modernism exhibition. Today, Rebajes's more unusual pieces can sell for hundreds of dollars.
Regel, A	Unknown	A REGEL 1/20 12K	The only Regel jewelry I have seen is large retro modern style brooches. These are typically made with colored and clear stones and marked A REGEL followed by the metal content.
Regency	1950 – 1970	REGENCY on oval cartouche; REGENCY JEWELS "Fleur de Paris by Regency"	Regency jewelry was made by the Regina Novelty Company of New York. Their jewelry is well designed and beautifully made using excellent quality materials and unusual stones. They are particularly well known for their butterfly brooches which are considered to be among the best ever made. Regency jewelry is available in the collectibles market and can be expensive.
Reinad	1922 – 1950s	Reinad 5th Av N.Y. SCEPTRON (1944) Chanel (1941 – not to be confused with Coco Chanel jewelry) REINAD NYC Reinad	Reinad Fifth Avenue made jewelry for other companies, including Boucher, Carnegie, and Eisenberg. They also had a retail novelty line named Chanel Novelty Co. which was short-lived because of a conflict with Coco Chanel jewelry which objected to the use of the name "Chanel." The jewelry that Reinad marketed was excellent quality using classic designs and top grade materials. It is rare in the collectible market. Jewelry marked SCEPTRON features classic 1940s retro designs and is made using sterling silver.

Selected Costume Jewelry Designers and Manufacturers

Manufacturer / Designer	Dates of Operation	Signature / Marks	Description / Characteristics
Reja	1941 – 1953	DEJA REJA REJA STERLING	Reja was founded by Solomon Finkelstein. The company began manufacturing jewelry for retail in 1939 under the name Deja but they were taken to court by DuJay. As a result they were required to change their name and in January 1941 they announced their new name "Reja." Designs included classic rhinestone brooches, enameled flowers, and some large and very well made figural jewelry. The elegantly designed jewelry was offered for sale in boutiques. Not all Reja jewelry was signed.
Renoir (Matisse) of California	1946 – 1964	Matisse Renoir Matisse (1952 – 1964) Sauteur (1958 – 1963) ©Renoir and a few others.	Renoir of California, Inc. was founded by Jerry Fels in 1946 and was headquartered in Los Angeles. (Fels also made mid-century modern wall sculptures under the name "JERE.") Matisse was founded a few years later in 1952. Both specialized in the manufacture of modern copper and enameled copper jewelry pins, clamper bracelets, earrings, and necklaces. The jewelry features modern designs using bright enamels in shades of white, black, green, and pale blue. The jewelry is available in the collectibles market. It is not unusual to find a brooch with or without matching earrings. However parures are more rare.
Richelieu	1911 – 2003	RICHELIEU on raised rectangle Richelieu Bill Smith of Richelieu (1970s) Richelieu Satinore Richelieu Iridelle Richelieu Pearls Before 1950s not all jewelry was marked.	Joseph H. Meyer & Bros. began producing jewelry with the Richelieu mark in Brooklyn, New York, in 1911. Between 1940 – 1960, they made necklaces and earrings with pearls, enamel pins, and rhinestone jewelry. They also made colorful Lucite sets. Richelieu jewelry is above average to excellent quality, featuring interesting designs, particularly enameled figurals.
Robert, Original by	1942 – 1979	Original by Robert Fashioncraft Fashioncraft Robert Robert	Fashioncraft Jewelry Co. was founded in New York City by Robert Levy, David Jaffee, and Irving Landsman. The company was noted for excellent enameling and rhinestone jewelry; it is sometimes confused with Miriam Haskell jewelry as it employs similar materials and techniques. It is uncommon in the collectibles market and can be expensive. Around 1960, the name was changed to Robert Originals, Inc. In 1979 the company was named Ellen Designs for Robert Originals (Ellen is the daughter of David Jaffee and joined the company in 1979). In 1984 the company became Ellen Designs.

Selected Costume Jewelry Designers and Manufacturers

Manufacturer / Designer	Dates of Operation	Signature / Marks	Description / Characteristics
Robert Rose	1945 – present	ROBERT Rose	Robert Rose jewelry is made by Jewelry Fashions, Inc. in New York.
Roma	1963 – unknown	ROMA©	Roma jewelry was made by Fairdeal Manufacturing Company in Providence, Rhode Island.
Roman	1973 – present	ROMAN	The Roman Company was founded in St. Louis, Missouri. They designed and distributed costume jewelry signed ROMAN. The company was purchased by TSI Holding Company in 1994; jewelry is now mainly manufactured in the Far East.
Rosenstein, Nettie	1935 – 1975	Nettie Rosenstein on raised rectangle STERLING Nettie Rosenstein	Nettie Rosenstein was a fashion designer and made jewelry to complement her fashions. Her jewelry is boutique quality and was often made with sterling and rhinestones. It featured traditional heraldic symbols with softer romantic designs resulting in an unusual and unique look. Also seen are Victorian designs incorporating cameos and rhinestones. It is rare, expensive, and highly collectible.
Sandor	1938 – 1972	SANDOR SANDOR© (after 1954) SANDOR CO.©	Sandor was founded by Sandor Goldberger. The company was known for beaded jewelry featuring elaborate designs which incorporated faux coral, pearls, and crystals. These pieces are rare. More commonly found are high quality enameled pins, especially the floral designs. Sandor was one of the first companies to feature enameled costume jewelry.
Sarah Coventry	1949 – 1984 also 2002 – 2003	©SARAH ©SARAHCOV SC, SAC, SaC on oval cartouche COVENTRY© and many others	Founded by Charles H. Stuart in 1949 and named for his granddaughter Sarah. Stuart also founded Emmons. Coventry jewelry includes a variety of styles and materials. It was sold mostly at home parties or given as contestant gifts on game shows and at beauty pageants. The company's excellent marketing strategies helped make Sarah Coventry a household name. Medium to better quality designs run the gamut from Victorian revival to classic and modern designs using rhinestones, gold-tone and silver-tone, and plastics. Home parties were discontinued in 1984 but started again in the 1990s. The company was sold to a Canadian firm in 1984.
Sceptron (See Reinad)		SCEPTRON (first used in 1944)	Reinad Novelty Co., Inc. and Sceptron jewelry creations formed a partnership resulting in jewelry marked SCEPTRON. Their retro modern designs feature excellent quality materials.

Selected Costume Jewelry Designers and Manufacturers

Manufacturer / Designer	Dates of Operation	Signature / Marks	Description / Characteristics
Schiaparelli, Elsa	1931 – 1973 (except for a period of time during WWII)	Early pieces were usually unsigned; may have Schiaparelli on raised rectangle. Later pieces are signed Schiaparelli on a cartouche (after 1949).	Schiaparelli jewelry features colorful rhinestones in excellent and beautiful designs. Her early abstract arrangements from the 1930s employed various stones and glass decorations and unconventional materials in outrageous designs. The later pieces are not as rare as those produced in France in the 1930s. Schiaparelli jewelry is popular with collectors. It is rare and expensive; unfortunately it has also been reproduced.
Schreiner	1939 – 1977	SCHREINER NEW YORK SCHREINER	The company was founded by Henry Schreiner who began his career in the 1920s with a company that manufactured shoe buckles. Schreiner jewelry was never mass produced. Intricate designs with characteristic use of rhinestones (inverted) have made Schreiner jewelry sought after by collectors. Early pieces were unsigned but savvy collectors are able to identify Schreiner jewelry.
Selini	1950s – 1960s	SELINI© on raised rectangle; some jewelry is marked with both names (Selro and Selini) Selini jewelry is not always marked and some pieces were marked with hang tags	Paul Selenger named the company after his mother Rose; Selro was first, followed by Selini in an attempt to differentiate the two. Selro is best known for figural jewelry featuring Asian and devil faces. It is very well made and highly collectible. Selini jewelry also features excellent quality classic rhinestone designs with enameled accents. Collectors enjoy both the figural jewelry and the more traditional designs. It is not particularly rare; one can almost always find an auction of signed or unsigned pieces on eBay.
Selro	1950s – 1960s	SELRO CORP© on raised rectangle	See Selini, above: best known for figural jewelry including Asian and devil faces; extremely well made and collectible and not always signed. They also featured excellent quality rhinestone jewelry.
Spinx	1950 – present	SPINX with design number or the number only	Spinx is a British firm founded in 1950 by S. Root in Chiswick. Spinx has made jewelry for K.J.L., Butler & Wilson, 5th Avenue, and others. Jewelry signed SPINX is rare in the collectibles market.
Star-Art	1940s (perhaps earlier) – 1960s	STAR-ART mark includes metal content	There is no reliable information available on Star-Art jewelry. The designs I have seen feature delicate floral designs in retro modern style settings with colorful rhinestones and curled metal.

Selected Costume Jewelry Designers and Manufacturers

Manufacturer / Designer	Dates of Operation	Signature / Marks	Description / Characteristics
St. Gielar, Ian	1989 – present	STANELY HAGLER NYC on an oval cartouche Ian St Gielar on an oval cartouche (both signatures on each piece)	Ian St. Gielar jewelry was individually made; each item was signed and numbered. All pieces were hand crafted and limited to six pieces of each design. The beautiful and colorful contemporary designs show the influence of Miriam Haskell and Stanley Hagler. His wife is continuing to make jewelry in the St. Gielar style, following Ian's untimely death in 2007.
Swarovski	1895 – present	S.A.L. SAWY Swan mark	Daniel Swarovski invented a machine in 1892 that could cut crystals. Daniel, brother-in-law Franz Weis, and Armand Kosmann founded Swarovski in 1895. Swarovski began making its own jewelry line in the late 1970s; as of January 2006 most production was in Asia and Europe. The company now sells through its own line of retail stores. Their jewelry features excellent quality and classic designs in gold-tone and silver-tone settings featuring what else? Clear and colored rhinestones!
Tara	1960s	TARA	Tara jewelry was sold at home parties, much like Sarah Coventry and Emmons. It featured colored rhinestones in gold-tone settings and rhinestones in thermoplastic jewelry designs. It is average quality and is becoming more readily available in the collectibles market. Tara Fifth Ave. jewelry moved from New York to California in the mid-1960s.
Taylord	1940 – unknown	TAYLORD 1/20 12K GOLDFILLED TAYLORD STERLING	Taylord jewelry was made in Newark, New Jersey. The designs I have seen are typically retro modern. I was unable to find any other reliable information on Taylord jewelry.

Selected Costume Jewelry Designers and Manufacturers

Manufacturer / Designer	Dates of Operation	Signature / Marks	Description / Characteristics
Trifari	1918 – present	There are many different marks for Trifari jewelry. The most commonly seen mark in the collectibles market is TRIFARI© with a small crown over the "T." See *Collecting Costume Jewelry 101* by Julia Carroll for a more complete list of Trifari marks.	Trifari made jewelry beginning in the mid-nineteenth century in Italy. Gustavo then came to U.S. in the early part of the twentieth century and after serving as a jewelry apprentice, he established Trifari costume jewelry. It was short-lived however lasting just two years. In 1917 Leo Krussman joined Trifari; by 1925, Trifari, Krussman, and Fishel was established. Alfred Philippe joined Trifari as chief designer in 1930 after having designed jewelry for Cartier. Trifari's brilliant marketing campaign, beginning in 1938, helped make it a household name. Philippe's original designs helped cement Trifari's reputation. Trifari jewelry features a wide variety of designs employing rhinestones, enamel, thermoplastic, faux gemstones, and pearls. Their sterling silver crowns and jelly belly pins are among the most famous and collectible of Trifari designs.
Van Dell	1938 – present	VAN DELL STERLING VAN DELL with metal content	Van Dell corporation was established in Providence, Rhode Island, in 1939. It was purchased by Colibri in 1991, who also owns Krementz. It is still being sold today. Van Dell designs typically featured floral, rhinestone, enameled pieces, and hand-carved ivory.
Vendome (Coro)	1944 – 1970	VENDOME VENDOME©	Coro's high end line of jewelry (Coro Craft) was replaced by Vendome. The chief designer for Vendome jewelry was Helen Marion. Designs feature high quality rhinestones and beads, rich enameling, and excellent metalwork. The jewelry is available in the collectibles market. Beaded necklace demi parures are more common than the elaborate enameled jewelry.
Vogue	1936 – 1975	VOGUE VOGUE STERLING Vogue Jlry	Vogue was founded by Harold Shapiro, Jack Gilbert, and George Grand. Their designs feature some figural pins as well as the more commonly found beaded jewelry. Earlier Vogue pieces (1930s – 1940s) are scare in the collectibles market.
Warner	1953 – 1971	WARNER on oval cartouche	Warner was founded and operated by Joseph Warner. The jewelry was made with brilliant rhinestones in outstanding floral, fruit, and insect designs. Japanned settings helped give Warner its distinctive look. It is very well made using excellent materials and is somewhat rare in the collectibles market.

Selected Costume Jewelry Designers and Manufacturers

Manufacturer / Designer	Dates of Operation	Signature / Marks	Description / Characteristics
Weiss	1942 – 1971	WEISSCO (first used in 1947) WEISS with © after 1955 A.W. Co with a large center letter W in the shape of a crown. Jewelry was also marked with hang tags	Albert Weiss founded the company in 1942, and also designed jewelry, having gained experience in the field when he worked for Coro. Michael Weiss continued to operate the company after his father's death. It ceased operations in 1971. Weiss jewelry designs include beautifully designed clear and colored rhinestone jewelry in gold-tone and japanned settings, plastic jewelry including fabulous colored plastic and rhinestone clamper bracelets, and enameled pieces, including some Christmas and flower jewelry. Weiss black diamond jewelry features smoky quartz-colored rhinestones in lovely and classic designs. Weiss jewelry is well made and available in the collectibles market. It is also possible to find Weiss vintage ads. Unfortunately, Weiss jewelry has been reproduced and is being sold on eBay and elsewhere. The copies are attractive but can be identified as copies by looking at the backs of brooches. The fakes have textured finished; authentic pieces have smooth finishes.
Whiting & Davis	1926 – 1991 They stopped producing non-mesh jewelry in 1980 and all jewelry in 1991.	Whiting & Davis Co. Bags	C.W. Whiting worked for a chain manufacturing company which was founded in 1876; he later became part owner and the company began producing jewelry in 1907. Best known for their mesh evening bags, Whiting & Davis also made excellent quality museum jewelry reproductions. Made in the 1950s, these sets are extremely popular with collectors. Whiting & Davis also made high quality silver-tone and gold-tone jewelry. Their necklace and bracelet sets usually feature a large center stone (faux gemstone or colored stone) in ornate settings. The mesh evening bags continue to be popular with collectors.
Wiesner, Joseph	1953 and perhaps earlier	JOSEPH WIESNER N.Y. on oval cartouche[3] [3] Some jewelry is marked "WIESNER"; it is not certain what company made this jewelry.	Joseph Wiesner jewelry features beautiful and well made clear and colored rhinestone jewelry, some in Art Deco designs. The 1960s *Jewelers' Buyers Guide* provides an address for Joseph Wiesner on 16 W. 37th St. in New York. Joseph Wiesner jewelry is somewhat rare in the collectibles market.

Bibliography

Aikins, Ronna Lee. *Brilliant Rhinestones Identification & Value Guide.* Collector Books, Paducah, KY, 2003.

———. *20th Century Costume Jewelry 1900 – 1980, Identification and Price Guide.* Collector Books, Paducah, KY, 2005.

Auerbach, George. *Antique Jewelry on Assembly Line: Modern Production Methods Are Used to Step Up Output of Baubles and Dangles.* New York Times, February 27, 1955.

Baker, Lillian. *50 Years of Collectible Fashion Jewelry, 1925 – 1975.* Collector Books, Paducah, KY, 1995.

Ball, Joanne Dubbs. *Costume Jewelers, the Golden Age of Design.* Schiffer Publishing, Ltd., Atglen, PA, 2000.

Becker, Vivienne. *Fabulous Costume Jewelry: History of Fantasy and Fashion in Jewels.* Schiffer Publishing, LTD., Atglen, PA, 1993.

Bell, C. Jeanne. *Warman's Antique Jewelry Field Guide.* Krause Publications, Iola, WI, 2003.

Brown, Marcia "Sparkles." *Coro Jewelry, A Collectors Guide.* Collector Books, Paducah, KY, 2005.

———. *Rhinestone Jewelry: Figurals, Animals, and Whimsicals, Identification and Values.* Collector Books, Paducah, KY, 2006.

———. *Signed Beauties of Costume Jewelry.* Collector Books, Paducah, KY, 2002.

———. *Unsigned Beauties of Costume Jewelry.* Collector Books, Paducah, KY, 2000.

Brunialti, Carla Ginelli and Brunialti, Roberto. *A Tribute to America: Costume Jewelry 1935 – 1950.* Publishing project by EDITA, Milan, January 2002.

Carroll, Julia C. *Collecting Costume Jewelry 101: The Basics of Starting, Building, and Upgrading.* Collector Books, Paducah, KY, 2004.

———. *Collecting Costume Jewelry 202: The Basics of Dating Jewelry 1935 – 1980.* Collector Books, Paducah, KY, 2007.

Cera, Deanna Farretti, ed. *Jewels of Fantasy.* Harry N. Abrams, Inc., New York, NY 1992 (This book accompanied the 1991 exhibition of the same name).

———. *Amazing Gems: An Illustrated Guide to the World's Most Dazzling Costume Jewelry.* Harry N. Abrams, Inc., New York, NY 1995.

Corwin, Susan Simon. *Irving Wolf and Trifari: A View from the Top.* VFCJ, Vol. 16, No. 3, 2006.

Costume Jewelry Again in Vogue; 'Big and Barbaric' Trinkets Rule. *New York Times,* November 25, 1933.

Costume Jewelry Due for Big Season, *New York Times,* June 21, 1944.

Costume Jewelry Gains; Sales in 1940 Exceeded 1939 Volume, Rosenberger Says. *New York Times,* January 4, 1941.

Davis, Carolyn N. *The Jewelry of Harry Iskin, Vintage Fashion & Costume Jewelry,* Vol. 16, No. 2, 2006.

DeLizza, Frank R. *Memoirs of a Fashion Jewelry Manufacturer.* DeLizza Publishing, 2007.

Dolan, Maryanne. *Collecting Rhinestone & Colored Jewelry,* Books Americana, Florence, AL, 1989.

Duke & Duchess of Windsor Society Quarterly Journal, *FAUX,* Issue 2, 2004.

Duval, Elizabeth R. New Things in City Shops: Costume Jewelry Runs Riot. *New York Times,* January 23, 1939.

Fashion: Jewelry Reflects Yesteryear and Orient: New Costume Pieces Contribute Sparkle and Bit of Luxury. *New York Times,* November 12, 1953.

Flood, Kathy. *Costume Jewelry Figurals,* Krause Publications, Iola, WI, 2007.

Hadley, Leila E. B. "Hey Daddy, I Want a Rhinestone Ring: Kenneth Jay Lane Makes Real Money Designing Fake Jewelry." *The Saturday Evening Post,* September 7, 1968, Vol. 241, Issue 18, pages 38 – 40.

Hafner, Katie. Seeing Fakes, Angry Traders Confront eBay. *New York Times,* January 29, 2006.

Hollie, Pamela G. Costume Jewelry Gains Status. *New York Times,* December 24, 1984.

Jewelers' Buyers Guide 1960, A. McKernin Publication, issued August 1959.

Bibliography

Jewelry Men Told to End Metal Use. *New York Times*, March 25, 1942.

Kelly, Lyngerda and Schiffer, Nancy. *Costume Jewelry – The Great Pretenders*, Revised 4th Edition. Schiffer Publishing Ltd., Atglen, PA, 1996.

Klein, Susan Maxine. *Mid-Century Plastic Jewelry*. Schiffer Publishing Ltd., Atglen, PA, 2005.

Lane, Kenneth Jay and Miller, Harrice Simmons, *Faking It*. Harry N. Abrams, Inc., New York, NY, 1996.

Leshner, Leigh. *Rhinestone Jewelry: A Price and Identification Guide*. Krause Publications, Iola, WI, 2003.

Lindbeck, Jennifer A. *Fine Fashion Jewelry From Sarah Coventry*. Schiffer Publishing Ltd., Atglen, PA, 2000.

Miller, Judith with Wainwright, John. *Costume Jewelry: The Complete Visual Reference and Price Guide*. DK Collector's Guides, London, New York, Melbourne, Munich, and Dehli, 2003.

Musetti, Katerina. *The Art of Juliana Jewelry*. Schiffer Publishing, Ltd., Atglen, PA, 2008.

New Costume Jewelry: Chanel's Gold Necklaces are Flamboyant—Iridescent Blue and Pink Angel Wings. *New York Times*, January 30, 1938.

Notes on Fashion. *New York Times*, September 17, 1985.

Pinch of War Felt in Novelty Exhibit, *New York Times*, February 5, 1942.

Pitman, Ann Mitchell. *Inside the Jewelry Box: A Collector's Guide to Costume Jewelry*. Collector Books, Paducah, KY, 2004.

———. *Inside the Jewelry Box, Volume 2*. Collector Books, Paducah, KY, 2007.

Proddown, Penny. Healy, Debra, and Fasel, Marion. *Hollywood Jewels: Movies, Jewelry, Stars*. Harry N. Abrams, New York, NY, 1992.

Reinitz, Bertram. New Our Jewels Are Synthetic: Stones, Glass, and Compositions of Metal Are Imported by American Manufacturing Jewelers and Turned Into Trinkets of Odd Styles. *New York Times*, January 27, 1929.

Rezazadeh, Fred. *Costume Jewelry – A Practical Handbook and Value Guide*. Collector Books, Paducah, KY, 1998 (values updated 2006).

Romero, Christie. *Warman's Jewelry: Identification and Price Guide*, 3rd Edition. Krause Publications, Iola, WI. 2002.

Salsbery, David & Lee. *ABCs of Costume Jewelry*. Schiffer Publishing, Ltd., Atglen, PA, 2003.

Schiro, Anne-Marie. *Costume Jewelry: Closer to the Real Thing*. *New York Times*, October 20, 1987.

Simonds, Cheri. *Collectible Costume Jewelry*. Collector Books, Paducah, KY, 1997.

Skidelsky, Sibilla. *Costume Gems for all Moods: New Art of Designing Jewels Aims at Giving Glamour with Every Dress*. *New York Times*, December 8, 1940.

Solis-Cohen, Lita, Editor. *The Americana Chronicles: 30 Years of Stories, Sales, Personalities, and Scandals from the Maine Antique Digest*. Running Press Publishers, Philadelphia, PA, 2004.

Sotheby's Sale Catalog: The Jewels of the late Duchess of Windsor, April 2 – 3, 1987.

Taylor, Elizabeth. *My Love Affair With Jewelry*. Simon and Schuster, 2003.

Tolkien, Tracy and Wilkinson, Henrietta. *A Collector's Guide to Costume Jewelry: Key Styles and How to Recognize Them*. Firefly Books, Canada, 1997.

Wolf, Madeline F. Women Make Jewelry an Accent in Costume. *New York Times*, February 23, 1930.

www.hattie-carnegie.com
www.illusionjewels.com
www.morninggloryjewelry.com
www.sparklz.com

Favorite Online Dealer Sites

Website www.Rubylane.com features a wide selection of well priced vintage jewelry from many dealers. Among my favorites are Boo Bears Baubles, Jewels by Liz, Kattslair, Mona Liza Jewelry, Our Attic's Treasures, Pie in the Sky, Splendors of the Past, Sunnyside Farms, Unforgettable, Vintage Vibe, Bella Sorella, Sweetie's Memorable Gemz, and Alison Phalan.

www.Sparklz.com
www.TACE.com
www.TIAS.com

Among my favorite antique shops are:
Aged to Perfection, Route 30, Elwood, NJ (An antique co-op featuring many dealers).

Pack Rat, 80 Mill Street, Mays Landing, NJ (Owners Bob and Mary Hahn feature a variety of new and vintage jewelry and other antiques).

Stuarts Draft Antique Mall, Route 340, Stuarts Draft, VA.

Index

A. J. C. 160, 162
Amco 20, 55, 162
Art 8, 22, 27, 66, 68, 72, 77, 84, 90, 91, 96, 101, 128, 129, 140, 142, 143, 147, 162
Atwood and Sawyer .. 23, 25, 95, 162
Austria, Made in 29, 30, 32, 48, 52, 108, 162
Avon 23, 25, 73, 93, 105, 127, 133, 159, 162
B. S. K. 22, 57, 60, 71, 77, 87, 100, 164
Bakelite 25
Barclay, McClelland 8, 21, 163
Beatrix 163
Beau Jewels 52, 54, 114, 163
Boucher, Marcel 8, 12, 21, 22, 25, 43, 56, 58, 84, 97, 163
Brand 150, 164
Brookraft 164
Butler 92, 164
Cadaro 22, 149, 164
Calvaire 20, 81, 164
Capri 22, 57, 73, 106, 165
Carl-Art 21, 59, 165
Carnegie, Hattie 6, 21, 34, 59, 60, 64, 94, 99, 101, 102, 112, 149, 165
Carolee 13, 23, 25, 165
Castlecliff 20, 84, 142, 166
Caviness, Alice 22, 72, 166
Celebrity 166
Ceno 78, 166
Cerrito 59, 166
Chanel, Coco 10, 20
Ciner 21, 108, 157, 166
Claiborne, Liz 58, 178
Colco 130, 167
Continental 155, 167
Coro 6, 16, 20, 23, 24, 37, 38, 59, 62, 80, 81, 82, 88, 98, 103, 117, 123, 138, 145, 150, 152, 156, 167, 187
Coro Craft 49
Coventry, Sarah 22, 26, 73, 83, 85, 88, 101, 104, 106, 113, 115, 116, 117, 121, 123, 124, 125, 136, 159, 184
Craft 16, 63, 133, 167
Craft (Gem-Craft) 22
Czechoslovakia 78, 168
Dalsheim 49, 168
De Nicola 23, 102, 168
DeLizza and Elster .. 22, 31, 35, 43, 44, 45, 64, 80, 101, 108, 122, 148, 154, 168
Di Niscemi, Mimi 23, 153, 180
Doddz 27, 38, 169
Dorset Fifth Avenue 157

Eisenberg 9, 16, 20, 21, 150, 155, 169
Eisenberg Ice 78
Elzac 10, 12, 13, 22, 92, 93, 95, 170
Emmons 22, 100, 170
Eugene 6, 22, 134, 170
Fashioncraft 184
Florenza 22, 29, 49, 63, 71, 72, 84, 86, 94, 104, 110, 144, 147, 171
Francois 71, 79
Garné 150, 171
Gem-Craft 167
Gerry's 63, 68, 84, 159, 171
Givenchy 142, 171
Gold Crown 172
Goldette 23, 86, 145, 147, 171
Graziano, Robert 34, 172
Green, Judith 65, 69, 172
Hagler, Stanley 33, 51, 172
Halbe 98, 172
Har 8, 9, 15, 27, 28, 58, 73, 85, 86, 91, 96, 100, 109, 114, 128, 129, 130, 131, 154, 155, 173
Haskell, Miriam 21, 25, 99, 173
Hobé 20, 58, 65, 78, 132, 136, 144, 173
Hollycraft 21, 52, 75, 112, 174
Hong Kong 25, 139, 150, 174
Iskin, Harry 80, 174
J. J. 68, 175
Japan 25, 145, 174
Jeanne 94, 102, 174
Jomaz 21, 179
Joseff of Hollywood .. 10, 21, 33, 175
Judy Lee 124, 175
Juliana 31, 35
Karu-Arke 22, 50, 123, 175
Kim 156, 175
Kramer 22, 32, 47, 57, 90, 134, 140, 150, 155, 176
Krementz 20, 116, 126, 176
La Roco 20, 103, 177
Laguna 22, 137, 176
Lane, Kenneth J. 8, 23, 24, 25, 102, 115, 152, 177
Ledo 20, 75, 177, 182
Les Bernard .. 23, 40, 143, 151, 177
Lisner 16, 20, 29, 80, 83, 145, 178
Mamselle 70, 178
Marvella 10, 20, 98, 99, 111, 143, 179
Matisse 82, 120, 132, 183
Mazer 21, 136, 150, 179
Mexico 22, 97, 179
Miracle 90, 180

Mode-Art 162
Monet 21, 61, 71, 82, 97, 149, 158, 180
Mylu 84, 180
Napier 12, 19, 20, 71, 128, 180
Newhouse 153, 181
Original by Robert 15
Pam 127, 181
Panetta 22, 67, 181
Park Lane 22, 153, 181
Pastelli 154, 181
Pell 22, 42, 73, 75, 84, 95, 101, 182
Polcini 75, 177, 182
Rebajes 21, 149, 182
Regel 80, 182
Regency 77, 86, 182
Reinad 21, 90, 91, 182, 184
Reja 21, 183
Renoir 22, 82, 183
Richelieu 20, 94, 95, 183
Robert Rose 79, 184
Robert, Original by 183
Roma 84, 100, 184
Roman 65, 184
Rosenstein, Nettie .. 21, 97, 141, 184
S. A. L. 160
Sandor 21, 57, 184
Sceptron 135, 184
Schaiparelli 21, 141, 185
Schreiner 6, 7, 21, 185
Selini 85, 113, 185
Selro Corp. 90, 148, 185
Spinx 73, 185
St. Gielar, Ian 23, 33, 51, 186
Star 32
Star-Art 117, 185
Staret 16
Sterling 58, 80, 119, 135, 146
Swarovski, Daniel 19, 20, 160, 186
Tara 147, 186
Taylord 22, 80, 186
Trifari 8, 16, 20, 24, 25, 37, 55, 66, 71, 90, 94, 103, 134, 144, 153, 187
Van Dell 21, 187
Vendome 22, 119, 141, 187
Vogue 21, 140, 187
Warner 22, 119, 155, 155, 187
Weiss 16, 22, 28, 30, 39, 45, 46, 48, 57, 58, 65, 74, 78, 87, 100, 101, 107, 109, 111, 115, 122, 138, 150, 151, 188
West Germany, Made in 73, 137, 171
Whiting and Davis 21, 133, 188
Wiesner 38, 46, 75
Wiesner, Joseph 22, 89, 188

Schroeder's ANTIQUES Price Guide

OUR #1 BEST-SELLER!

FULL COLOR!

#1 BESTSELLING ANTIQUES PRICE GUIDE

≈ More than 50,000 listings in over 500 categories
≈ Histories and background information
≈ Both common and rare antiques featured

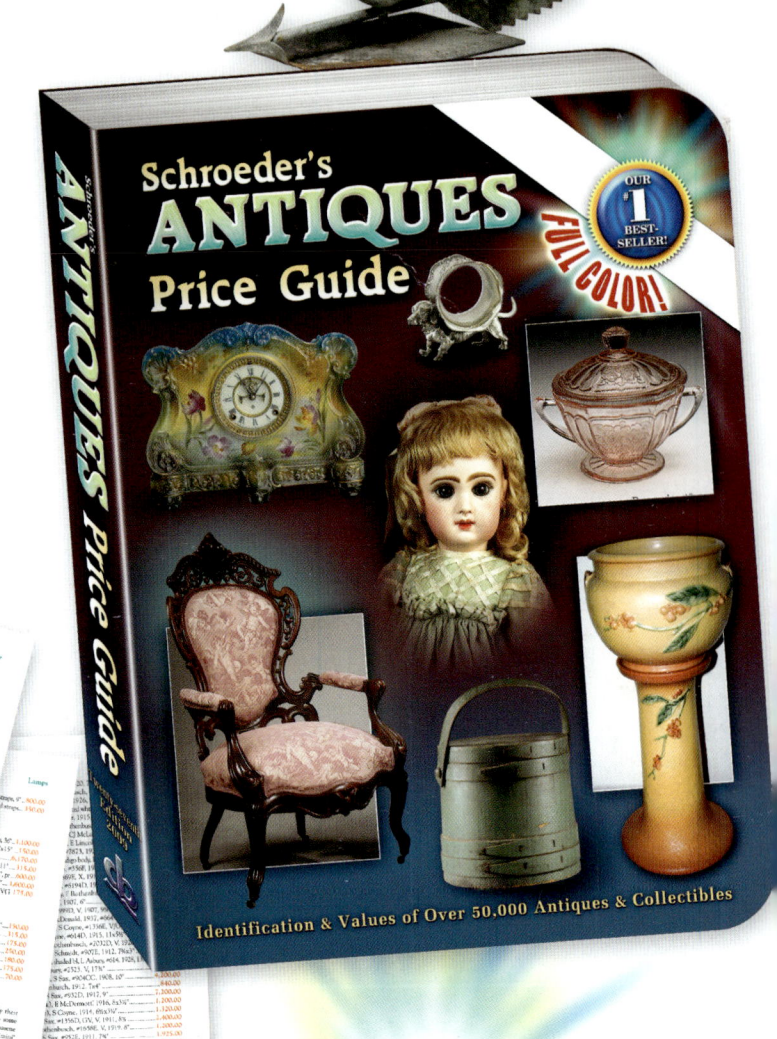

only **$19.95**
608 pages

COLLECTOR BOOKS
P.O. BOX 3009, Paducah KY, 42002-3009

1.800.626.5420

www.collectorbooks.com